How to Succeed With Your Great Business Idea

Smart Strategies for Entrepreneurs

By Doug Hickok

Illustrations by Leslie McGrath

Copyright © 2015 by Doug Hickok / Business Breakthrough, LLC. All rights reserved. This book or any portion thereof may not be reproduced or used in any manner whatsoever without the express written permission of the publisher except for the use of brief quotations in a book review.

Introduction

You have a great new business idea, something so perfect for you that it lights you up and puts a grin on your face.

Your idea is compelling, a dream that could set you free in many ways. This is big, isn't it? This could put you in control of your time, your choices, your future, and your life.

So, what happens next?

Do you know what to *do* with this idea, how to translate it into a successful business?

Many people think the first step toward starting a new business is to immediately get ready to open one, but it's not. You need to know a lot more before you open your doors. Otherwise, the foundation of your business will be weak, leading to various ongoing problems over time that will keep eating at your business like termites in a tree.

How do you set it up? What are the right steps? How much money will you need?

Do you know whether your idea will work? Can it give you a stable life and the rewards you desire?

How will you gain enough confidence in this idea that you can move forward with it clearly and strongly?

When you read this book, you will come to know the answers to all these questions, plus many more that you haven't even thought of yet.

You will also know the worth of your idea, both to you and in the marketplace where you will sell it.

Most importantly, you will have a more accurate picture of what you are getting into, and once you do act, you'll know what you're doing.

Dance instructors sometimes place cut-outs of steps on the floors of their studios to help students learn a particular dance step sequence. This book will give you "steps on the floor" to follow as you explore what your business idea would look like in action, and what it would need to be stable and successful.

So here's to you and your great business idea! How wonderful that it has arrived. Before you act, take time to learn about it, poke it and prod it, and develop the concept. Then, once it feels right, you'll be prepared to go for it.

Master Goal: Prepare to turn your great idea into an actual business.

Keyword: Learn

Inside Priority: Get clear before you act

Outside Priority: Do your research

Biggest Challenge: Boiling down all the possibilities into a single clear focus

Strengths at this stage: Ideas, energy, passion, enthusiasm

Possible weaknesses at this stage: Limited business experience or skills, being swept off your feet by the excitement of it all, difficulty staying focused, impatience, impulsivity, and acting prematurely

Smartest thing you need to do: Leverage the resources, skills, experience, and knowledge of others whenever possible

At this stage your business is: A galaxy of ideas whirling around inside your head

At this time you are: Pumped

Worst thing you'd never do: Start your business without preparing well for it

Your mantra at this stage: Slow down and do it right!

Table of Contents

Introduction i
This book is about how to decide whether to turn your Great Business Idea into a real business.

<u>Topics</u>

The Seven Steps of an Entrepreneur's Business 1
Your path to success, one step after another.

Start Your Own Business? 7
Your business starts inside of you with dreams and plans in your head and your heart.

The False Line Between "Business" and "Personal" 13
That dividing line is not always a good thing.

What's the Big Idea? 17
Guess where great business ideas come from?

But First, the Real Meaning of Money 24
It's not what you think it is.

How Ideas Turn into Money 30
Here's what you have to do.

Why Money Isn't Everything 35
There's a lot going on that feeds a need for money.

How Your Beliefs About Money Make You Rich or Poor 41
A couple of beliefs can ruin your entire money life, or make it hum.

How You Can Change Beliefs That Are Stopping You 44
Change your beliefs? Here's how to do it.

Why Money Is Everything 50
Sometimes in business, cash is king.

So You Want to Be an Entrepreneur 55
Are you qualified to do that?

Just Plan Confusing 61
Starting a business without a plan is risky, but what kind of plan do you need?

Getting Rid of the Boss? Not So Fast 63
Liberation has its trade-offs.

Falling in Love with Your Big Idea 68
Love is grand, but it can also lead you astray.

The Business Part of Owning a Business 73
You have to know some business before your dream can happen.

The Mixed Blessings of Business Partnerships 80
They can make you, and they can break you.

Why Partnering with Family and Friends Can Be Trouble 88
Watch relationships collide! Never speak to each other again!

Strategic Partners Are Money in the Bank 95
Multiply your sales through business-to-business referrals.

How Do You Know That Your Great Idea Will Work? 99
Start by specializing in something.

The Best Way to Stand Out Over the Competition 103
This has to happen for you to succeed.

What Is Your Market? 107
It takes three things to define your market.

Market Research—Not as Boring as It Sounds 113
How does what you offer fit into the marketplace?

What Is Your Compelling Value Proposition? 118
Why will people choose to buy from you instead of someone else?

Who Is Going to Sell What Must Be Sold? 122
You don't have a business unless you sell something.

Can You Make a Living That Meets Your Income and Lifestyle Needs? 127
Too many businesses struggle. Here's how you can avoid that.

What Do You Bring to the Table? **133**
It turns out you have a lot of success factors already in place.

Don't Get Killed by the Internet **140**
The World Wide Web presents a huge opportunity, and it is also a business killer.

How to Pass the Technology Test **143**
The digital technology revolution: love it or get left in the dust.

Who Is Along for the Ride? **146**
Nobody builds a business alone. Who is there (or not there) for you?

It's Time for Action **149**
You know which way to go. Really, you do.

A Word About Fear **151**
It's not fun when you feel it, but it has a positive purpose.

Go for It—Yes or No? **153**
How will you make this decision?

Congratulations! Now What? **158**
Now that you are going to start your business, here's what comes next.

How to Succeed With Your Great Business Idea

Smart Strategies for Entrepreneurs

By Doug Hickok

The Seven Steps of an Entrepreneur's Business

Entrepreneurs do not have much time to read big books. They usually read things that are useful and get to the point quickly because they are really busy. If you are thinking of becoming an entrepreneur, you probably fit this mold, and that is why this book is practical and short.

The question that comes up at some point for every would-be entrepreneur is this: "I have a really great business idea, but if I invest all the time, money, and risk that are needed to make an actual business out of it, will it succeed?"

This book gives you a process to look at your business idea and get a good sense of what it would take to bring it to life as an operating company.

By the time you finish the book, you will be clear about how you want to proceed in that direction.

This book was born out of my experience as an executive coach. I work with entrepreneurial leaders of small companies (fewer than 250 employees) every day, assisting them with support and structure so they can build the businesses they want and live the lives they want to live.

I have watched the evolution of these entrepreneurs and their successful businesses close-up over time, and I've noticed that there is a repeating progression to healthy business growth, a discernable series of steps that successful owners take as they start, operate, and grow those businesses.

Many entrepreneurs are not aware of the existence or continuity of those steps—seven of them—and as a result, their business growth journey is likely to have a lot of unnecessary ups and downs in it.

Wouldn't it be nice to know what you need to be doing at each step along the way—exactly what will shape your company to become what you want it to be?

Here are the seven steps.

Step One:
The Idea (What to do with your great business idea?)
Biggest challenge: Getting all relevant information so you can decide whether or not this idea will work as a real business if you do it

Step Two:
Startup (Setting up and opening your business)
Biggest challenge: Inadequate planning and preparation

Step Three:
Viability (Ongoing survival)
Biggest challenge: Making ongoing sales to support basic expenses and needs

Step Four:
Targeted Growth (Grow to thrive)
Biggest challenge: Coordinating all parts of your business so they grow together

Step Five:
Real Business (Owner independence)
Biggest challenge: Getting key people, systems, and infrastructure in place so you don't have to be there

Step Six:
Grow Big (Scale up)
Biggest challenge: Having enough cash and borrowing power

Step Seven:
Niche Dominance (Achievement of goals, abundant cash and revenues)
Biggest challenges: Getting stale and slow, growing away from core strengths

This book focuses on what you'll need to make good decisions about starting a business that would be based upon your business idea.

What *could* you do with that idea? It is both real and nebulous—how would you build a business from that? How do you begin to make sense of it and test it to get a glimpse of what it might look like as your actual day-to-day passion and working life? How can you get a real feel for whether starting this business would be worth your while and whether it would make you happy?

Read this book, and you will discover how to:

- Develop a clear picture of what your business would be like to start and run

- Define what the market is for what you offer. Who are the customers who make up your market, and how do you get them to show up and buy when you open your doors?

- Get a good sense of what will be needed for the business side of your company—all the practical stuff that needs to be done to keep everything else humming along

- Discover the strengths you already have that you can bring to your company—the abilities, perceptions, and wisdom that would give it a better chance of success

- Use the links in this book to tap all kinds of resources to help you on your way

There are reasons that more new businesses fail than succeed, and the main reason is that many business owners jump in quickly with a lot of hope and enthusiasm but not much of a grasp of the realities they are getting into. They wing it, and winging it involves too much guesswork and not enough practical foundation to create a steady, lasting, profitable business.

If you start that way, you will find yourself going in circles through constant trial-and-error activity to find out what works for you, because without a real structure and a plan, everything is an experiment. Trying things out all the time leads to a lot of dead ends that waste time and money.

Without a good foundation, there will be gaps in the way you start your business that will have implications that live on and magnify in your daily operations as you go forward. Errors and omissions will continue to restrict you and your business over time until you fix them. Once you realize you have a longstanding problem, you will spend a lot of time and money rooting out all of its effects and correcting things that could have been set up better in the beginning.

You can avoid all that if you start your business right.

Just as you would not want to operate an airplane without first learning how to fly, it is not a good idea to launch a business you have never run before until you have a really good sense of whether or not it will "fly."

This book is a way to find out about that, and you can begin now.

Read the book, take notes, and go talk to some successful entrepreneurs who are already doing what you want to do or something related. Then decide how to approach starting your own business.

Doug Hickok

Start Your Own Business?

When you start a business, there is so much to do!

Choose a product or service to sell, find out if anybody will buy it, raise a lot of cash, make a lot of plans, find a place, buy all kinds of stuff for the place, talk to many people, maybe hire some of them, figure out how to sell what you've got, decide who does what and what needs to be done, and pay the attorney, the city license people, and everyone else who helps along the way…

But wait a minute!

Before you *do* any of that, a lot of stuff has to get sorted out in your head, your heart, and your gut. Before you leap into action, you also have to think, and plan, and figure out how everything fits together so the actions you take are appropriate and effective.

You've got to put your business together inside of you, and then you can build it on the outside. Starting and running a business is an inside/outside process., and both parts need to work together to have a chance at success.

If you play the guitar, that guitar is the instrument that takes the music inside of you and gives it to the world in a way that connects you with people.

When you start a new business, you are the instrument that gives your business a unique life in the world through all the choices you make about it.

You choose: My company will sell this thing instead of that thing. We sell it this way instead of that way. This is how we will be different from every other business of our kind. I will hire this person instead of that person. I will sell to this market instead of that market.

And so it goes, decision after decision—you, giving shape to your business dream, just as a guitar gives sound to the inner music.

In the excitement of your new river of business ideas, you will often be tempted to jump into a lot of actions without thinking or feeling them through very well. You will be tempted to act in the world without an adequate inner foundation of thought, feeling, and preparation because you are so excited.

This book is not a glorified to-do list, a long checklist of actions you should take to start and run your business. That would put way too much emphasis on action and not nearly enough attention on your inner foundation—you-the-instrument preparing for action.

There are plenty of books out there that mainly focus on the outer activities of starting a business.

In this book, we will pay equal attention to inside *and* outside so you can be strong enough and wise enough to resist the seduction of action for its own sake, for the rush, for the feeling that you're getting somewhere even when you're not.

Here are some definitions:

> Inside: The inner life in you—the dreaming, imagining, and thinking factory in your mind, heart, and gut—the place where inner guidance, dreams, thoughts, emotions[1], and desires come together to give your business invisible shape before it takes physical form in the outer world. In the context of this book, "inside" means the imagining, thinking, feeling, intuitive[2] parts of building and running your business.
>
> Outside: The world of your physical senses—the place of physical action and implementation; creation in the material world. In the context of this book, "outside" means the out-in-the-world, action parts of building and running your business.
>
> Inside/out: Ideally, insight (inside) and action (outside) together form a balanced feedback loop, with enough insight onboard to guide action and enough action performed to provide real-world feedback that triggers further insight. Your feeling, thinking, imagining[3], and intuiting inner self needs to work smoothly with your physical action-in-the-world self to produce a vibrant, focused, coherent business.

---

[1] http://www.wired.co.uk/news/archive/2014-01/02/mapping-body-emotions
[2] http://www.psychologytoday.com/blog/the-intuitive-compass/201108/what-is-intuition-and-how-do-we-use-it
[3] http://dictionary.reference.com/browse/imagination

This is similar to how two different lenses in a pair of eyeglasses combine their individual slices of vision to produce a single, complete view.

You can build a business with a lot of action and a dollop of insight, but it's a lot like having only one good eye—the result will be limited and flawed, and there will be blind spots everywhere. Then when challenging times come along, the blind spots will sink you before you know it.

To grow your business to last requires that you be mostly balanced in your inner-outer loop. When you have that balance, a rich variety of options appear during good times and bad, instead of limited options that focus mostly or reflexively upon action as the default way to get through everything.

A balance of inside/outside will save you during hard times. During good times, that balance will build you a better business than your competition, and that inner synergy will provide you with the margin between just getting by and being a big success.

Here is what the movement of a balanced loop between inner and outer self looks like as you create and direct your business over time:

Dream > Imagine > Think > Act >
Action feedback > Adjust > Dream > Imagine > Think > Act again…

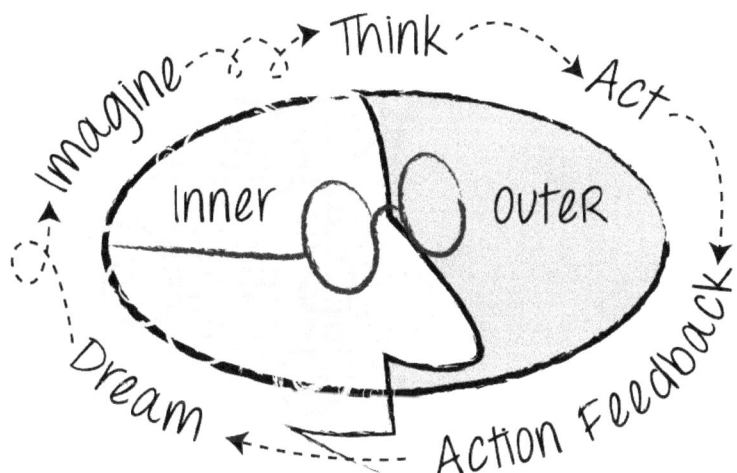

This is a cycle that should robustly continue for the life of your business.

Here's another way to look at it:

One way to imagine this process is to see it as an airplane. It is obvious from the illustration that the airplane needs both wings in order to fly, just as you need both sides of yourself in your business so it—and you—can move forward and thrive.

Doug Hickok

The False Line Between "Business" and "Personal"

For a long time, there has been a reigning erroneous belief in American business that we could and should somehow separate our professional selves from our personal selves. We're supposed to be all business at work and leave everything personal at home.

We are now beginning to understand that people can't be separated out into their constituent personality parts in order to be more effective at work. Trying to deny your personality at work doesn't make you better at work—it deprives you of personal tools and perspectives that allow you to work better wherever you are.

Of course, there need to be boundaries at work about how you behave and how many personal life activities you engage in, but try telling that to any manager who attempts to limit employee use of Facebook on company time!

Within human beings, there are no separate compartments labeled "professional" and "personal." We are not limited to having business thoughts at work and personal thoughts at home, and it is completely unrealistic and unreasonable to expect that we would operate that way.

It is when the professional and the personal are working well together, just like our inside and outside, that we achieve our highest potential for performance in business.

Leave out either of those parts, though, and you are crippled.

So, as we look into how to start, run, and grow your business, we will be looking at it from all these dimensions—inside and outside, professional and personal—because they each have a critical role to play.

Where to begin?

Since every new business begins with an idea, that's where we will start, but first, here are some ways to put these concepts into action.

Take action for traction: *How you can put the topic you just read into action?*

Think about the concept of inside/outside balance as you consider these action steps:

- How balanced are you between inside and outside, between preparation and action? Place a mark on the scale. Don't think too much about it; just go from your gut.

    Inside – 0 0 0 0 0 0 0 0 0 0 – Outside

- The one thing you could do to increase your inner/outer balance the most is:

    _____

    _____

- Will you act upon this one thing, and if so, how and when? Please be very specific.

  _____
  _____
  _____

As you consider these action items, think about any spoken or unspoken workplace rules about how you must leave your personal life at home when you come to work.

- When you consider the positions you have held, either working for yourself or someone else, what parts of your personal self did you end up leaving at home? Who are you at home that you can't be at work? Make a list of those qualities and characteristics.

  1. _____
  2. _____
  3. _____

- When you have made your list, decide which part you miss the most when you're at work.

  _____
  _____

- How could you appropriately take some of that valuable personal self to work, and how might doing that contribute to the quality and enjoyment of your work?

  _____

  _____

Doug Hickok

What's the Big Idea?

When people get ideas about starting a new business, those ideas[4] range from inspired to weird.

- Monks start a discount printing ink business[5] because they can't find replacement ink for their printer at a reasonable price.

- The people at *Airbnb* come up with an app to connect parking-starved motorists[6] with private citizens willing to rent their empty driveways by the hour.

- A happily married man starts a dating website for cheaters that has over three million members.

Ideas are limitless, and you can be smitten by THE big idea for your business anywhere and at any time.

By the way, even if you already have your big idea for your business, keep reading because you're going to need a lot more great ideas to build it and run it right.

Wouldn't it be nice if there were a drive-in window for great business ideas? Actually, there is a next best thing. In all the stories I've heard from entrepreneurs over the years about how they got their great ideas, there are some common themes.

---

[4] http://dictionary.reference.com/browse/idea
[5] http://www.monksink.com/
[6] http://www.psfk.com/2013/07/rent-empty-driveways-parking.html

Some of the most commonly reported situations in which people get their great ideas are:

- In the shower
- Walking the dog
- Driving
- Daydreaming
- Writing a journal entry
- Awakening

If you ask people where ideas come from, they usually say, "From my mind."

Yet, if you try to actually think up ideas with your mind, it can be hard work because ideas are sneaky. They often don't come from the conscious thinking part of the mind. Even when you generate your idea through a brainstorming session, the conversation usually does not start with the idea itself, but rather with a topic that stimulates the idea to appear.

Ideas come from your unconscious mind[7], a deeper level that is below your thinking mind. You can't really go there and get ideas-on-demand because it's *unconscious* — your conscious mind can't see into it directly.

---

[7] http://www.forbes.com/sites/nickmorgan/2013/04/23/why-you-should-listen-to-your-unconscious-mind-and-what-it-can-tell-you/

So if your thinking mind can't just consciously dig up a bushel of yummy ideas at any old time, how can you get great ideas when you need them?

My dog Toby, a big yellow Lab, will show you how.

Toby loves everything water, and he *really* loves to play and fetch in a pond or lake. I throw the bright orange ball, and he swims out and brings it back; repeat for hours.

We usually play with the ball in the country at a pond that has a nice, thick layer of mud on the bottom. When I throw the ball into the water near the shore, Toby launches himself on top of it with a mighty splash. Then, because his 85-pound airborne power landing drives the ball into the mud, it is nowhere to be seen.

When Toby first experienced this disappearance of the ball, he would charge back and forth, water and mud flying everywhere as he tried very hard to find it. Sometimes he got lucky and it popped up, but most of the time he came up empty.

Toby is a smart dog, so he figured out a better tactic. He learned to just sit and wait for the ball to come up. He sits down in the water, in the mud, and unless he's sitting directly on the ball, it always comes up sooner or later because it's full of air and the mud is gooey enough that it just rises after a while.

Ideas are like that ball. If you charge around trying to find one, you often just muddy the waters and come up empty.

Here's how to get great ideas using the Toby Method.

1. Get very clear about what you want the idea to do. "I need a new killer software product" or "I need a new way of making a living."

2. Think about what you need for a while and see what kinds of ideas you come up with. Give it a shot. Remember, Toby got lucky sometimes when he stirred up the bottom through his own efforts.

3. But if that doesn't work, do the human version of Toby's sit-and-wait: take your attention off the need for an idea—go to the beach, read a book, or better yet, get in the shower or take a walk. Distract your mind so the idea can appear.

When you look at my list of the most common places where people get ideas, the thinking mind is on autopilot in all those situations.

Decades ago, I owned a magazine, and my partner, Michael, who understood the truth about ideas and money, used to patiently listen to me as I related my latest need, my latest anguish about the problem of the day.

When I finished, he would say, "Take the afternoon off and go to the lake" or "Go to a movie and think about it later."

Doug Hickok

At first that drove me nuts, but then I realized he was not telling me to be lazy about my work—he was telling me to turn off my trapped mind so ideas could appear.

Distract or quiet your mind after you are clear about what you want, and ideas will come up like bubbles in a glass of champagne.

Then the next natural question that arises when your great idea appears is, "What do I do with this idea now that I have it?"

First, since this is about business[8], let's take a look at what money has to do with ideas. If you don't get your head straight about money, you will blow your opportunities, no matter how many good ideas you have.

Take action for traction: *How can you put the topic you just read about into action?*

Think back and remember some great ideas you've had in your life as you work with these action items:

- What are the three best ideas you have had in your life?

    1. _____
    2. _____
    3. _____

- Did those ideas have anything in common, either in the way they came to you or in terms of what they were about? If so, what was common to all of them?

    _____
    _____
    _____

---

[8] http://www.investopedia.com/terms/b/business.asp

- What has been your best, most successful experience of putting one of your ideas into action, and what were the key factors that created your success? In other words, what had to happen to make it all work?

  _____
  _____
  _____
  _____

- If you were to start the business you're thinking of, how could you use these key factors that have already worked for you to be successful this time?

  _____
  _____
  _____
  _____

The quickest road to greater success is to identify success factors that have worked for you before and to build them into what comes next. Duplicating success is much easier than inventing it.

But First, the Real Meaning of Money

What is money?

I mean, really, beyond the fact that on the outside it's a piece of paper[9] or a bit of metal, what is money?

I have asked this question to thousands of people in training groups over the years, and many of them will usually say things like, "freedom" or "time off" or "a good retirement."

Those are a few of the things you can do with money, but they are not what money *is*.

"What does it represent?" I ask those groups. "What does that paper or coin represent?"

"Value," someone will answer.

"What kind of value?" I ask.

"The value of things and services," someone may say.

I say, "You're getting warmer. What is underneath every thing or service… where are they born from?"

Then we go back and forth until somebody gets down to the truth of it.

Every thing or service ever invented started with an idea.

---

[9] http://www.pbs.org/wgbh/nova/ancient/history-money.html

Henry Ford had an idea: put four wheels together with a frame and an engine, and away we go. The outworking of that idea created one of the most successful products of all time.

Alexander Graham Bell had an idea: what if we could transmit the sound of a human voice over a wire? Hello, data technology.

Everything starts with an idea.

What is money?

Money most fundamentally represents ideas.

Money gives us a physical symbol that we can hand back and forth to each other that represents the kind of value we place upon objects and services, and because objects and services are born out of ideas, that valuation is also and most fundamentally about the ideas themselves.

Start with an idea, and end up with money for it.

When you buy groceries, a house, a car, a suit, a pair of shoes, a massage, or a tune-up for your car, when you buy *anything*—you are voting with your money for those things and services, but at the core, you are also voting for the ideas they came from.

Somebody designed that car, that haircut, the size and shape of your house. The design was the expression of their idea, so at the bottom of it, money is all about ideas, and a lack of money is usually about idea constipation.

Instead of trying to figure out how to make more money when we don't have enough of it to meet our needs, we need to be figuring out how to have more and better ideas, which will produce all the money we need or want if we carry them forward and implement them wisely.

Seeing ourselves as trapped by a lack of money causes depression and anxiety as we scramble around the walls of our minds looking for a way through. When we take our minds off the money and focus more on ideas, those trapped feelings quickly give way to enthusiasm, energy, and creativity.[10]

"So, if money comes from ideas, how many ideas can you have?" I ask my group.

"An unlimited number!" they yell back, getting into it now.

"If there is no limit to the number of ideas you can have, and if money comes from ideas, how much money can you have?"

Things get quiet as the group digests this.

"An infinite amount of money?" someone asks.

---

[10] http://inventors.about.com/od/creativity/f/What-Is-Creativity.htm

"That's right," I say. "There is no limit to the amount of money you can have since there is no limit to the number of ideas you can have. And, by the way, there is never an actual shortage of money—the government prints money[11] in a basement in Washington!"

Silence.

"But ideas don't just turn into money," someone will say.

"No, of course not. You have to take them and build something with them that can be sold."

Still.

The base—the root of all stuff and services—is ideas.

So if money is about ideas, what is this thing we call "work" all about?

In its truest definition regarding business, work is the process we use to make an idea into something we can sell. This includes all the activities that are necessary to bring a product or service to market and sell it.

When it comes to money and work, most people see their path as working for others—getting a job. They choose to invest their time, energy, and ideas into representing and expanding upon other people's ideas.

---

[11] http://www.moneyfactory.gov/uscurrency/howmoneyismade.html

Go to work in a department store, a factory, a hair salon, or a dentist's office. Become a therapist, a doctor, or a lawyer. If you are stepping into a predetermined role on a well-worn path, your work is about representing someone else's ideas.

The salesman who sells Ford cars, and everyone whose work connects to Ford Motor Company, from auto designers to factory workers to the truck driver who delivers the cars, is supporting Henry Ford's original idea. They add their own value to it in the many ways they help those cars get to market and into customers' hands.

Having said that, here's an important, applicable law of money: the closer you are to the original idea, the more money you will make.

Henry Ford[12] became incredibly wealthy because he was the source of the great idea, and he was also the inventor of the physical car that came from his idea. The car salesman, on the other hand, makes a lot less money because he or she is far removed from Henry and his idea.

Sam Walton, who started Walmart, became one of the wealthiest men in the world, but the cashiers who work at your neighborhood Walmart store don't make much money.

Sam Walton and Henry Ford were entrepreneurs—people who had ideas of their own that they wanted to bring to

---

[12] http://www.history.com/topics/henry-ford

life instead of working for someone else, and in both cases, their ideas were original.

Entrepreneurs to this day want a shot at the great abundance and opportunity that can come from putting something on the market that starts with a great idea. They want to be American success stories.

How Ideas Turn into Money

There are two basic ways to turn ideas into money: start with your own original idea or do something that builds upon the ideas of others.

There were television interview show hosts before Oprah Winfrey[13], for example, but her caring personality and her very personal version of a daytime interview show mesmerized millions of people and made her one of the wealthiest women ever.

Steve Jobs[14] did not invent the first music player, but his music player was such a radical improvement over all the others that it became a core idea all its own. His simple, clean computer devices captured the high-end market in his field.

Oprah Winfrey and Steve Jobs took other people's ideas and added their own ideas to them in such fundamentally powerful ways that the ideas became new again. The previously ordinary afternoon interview show became *Oprah*, and the ordinary cassette tape player became the iPod.

Mary Kay Ash[15] turned the world of cosmetics on its head with her company, Mary Kay Cosmetics. What had been a cosmetics industry of the elite was opened up to any woman with ambition and drive. More than 100,000 women

---

[13] http://www.cnn.com/2013/08/05/us/oprah-winfrey-fast-facts/
[14] http://www.boomsbeat.com/articles/13/20131231/50-facts-that-you-didnt-know-about-steve-jobs.htm
[15] http://www.biography.com/people/mary-kay-ash-197044

have won the right, through their high sales levels, to earn a good living and drive a pink car from Mary Kay.

We also have our national hero entrepreneurs.

Benjamin Franklin[16] was America's most famous early entrepreneur. He was a printer, an author, an inventor, and a very good businessman who knew how to get products from his ideas made and marketed.

Thomas Edison[17] was another of our most talented and prolific inventors. Contrary to popular belief, he did not invent the light bulb, but he built one that was safe. He also designed the entire circuit system that housed the bulbs, and he went on to become the prime mover in the creation of our national electric utility industry.

Do you see the pattern? All these entrepreneurs had at least one great core idea, followed by a steady stream of other ideas that created and added value to the original idea, for which people would gladly and continuously pay.

Making good ideas real and bringing them successfully to market—that's what entrepreneurs do to create a successful business. The sky is the limit when they hit a big one.

But how can you tell a good idea from all the others? How do you know which idea to pursue, and what do you do with that idea once you think it's a winner?

---

[16] http://www.todayifoundout.com/index.php/2013/05/ben-franklin-facts/
[17] http://www.neatorama.com/2008/02/11/10-fascinating-facts-about-edison/#!xN6Xt

In 1975 Gary Dahl was in a bar listening to his friends complain about their pets. This gave him the idea for a "pet rock"—an actual rock—which would make no demands, require no feeding or attention, no visits to the vet.

Gary was a creative guy with a marketing background, so new ideas cascaded from his initial thought, and he knew right away how to turn those ideas into a product.

He wrote a very funny instruction manual on the care and training of a pet rock that was full of puns and fun. He put the manual, along with a small river rock nestled in straw, inside a box with breathing holes in it and made a million-and-a-half dollars in sales over the holiday season.

This is a good illustration of a specific product where it is very obvious that the idea is actually the product. Small river rocks have very little intrinsic value, but a spoof like this is good enough to sell.

Gary Dahl's idea worked out so well with the pet rock because he knew what to do with the original idea to get it to market, but the odds of this kind of immediate huge success for most new products and businesses are very low. That's one of the reasons you hear such discouraging statistics about the high rate of failure for business start-ups.

The world is full of people who have great ideas about awesome products and services. True! But the start-up boneyard is so vast because most people have no background in *business*—they don't have Gary Dahl's experience—and they don't know the processes needed to move their ideas from their minds to the marketplace in ways that can succeed.

Take action for traction: *How can you put the topic you just read about into action?*

Think back and remember how you made money in your life as you work with these action items:

- What ideas of yours have brought you money (ideas that have produced money in any amount at any time or place in your life)?

    _____

    _____

    _____

    _____

- What is the single most important *positive* thing about ideas and money that you learned from those experiences?

    _____

    _____

- In what way could you carry this learning forward into any new business venture you might start?

  _____

  _____

  _____

  _____

- What business experience and skills do you have that might help you in a business venture?

  _____

  _____

  _____

  _____

Why Money Isn't Everything

Before you enter into a business, it is important to be very clear about why you would be doing it. The "why" behind your business is the deepest motivator you will have to keep you going through the years—through the good times and the bad times.

It is important that your reason for being in business is a deep, strong one that will stand the test of those challenges.

For some people, making lots of money is their big reason, their big goal.

There is nothing inherently wrong with having the accumulation of money as a major goal for your business, but how well you will do with that depends upon how emotionally invested you are in the money. It takes deep feeling about your "why" to support you emotionally through all the headwinds you will encounter while growing your company.

People often assign emotions to money that in truth have more to do with other things. They think they want more money, when what they really want most deeply are the things they believe money would allow them to have.

Here is an example of that dynamic.

One day I was teaching a class about setting goals, and one of the attendees was a man—we'll call him Martin—who had a heartfelt desire to live on the type of fine estate usually occupied by the extremely wealthy. He could see himself there, and he could feel it. It was a very compelling vision for him.

When we reached the part of the class where everyone was writing down their goals, he raised his hand and asked for help.

"When I write down my goal to live on a beautiful estate, I feel depressed because I make nine dollars an hour, and there's probably no way I will ever have the money to buy that estate and live that dream."

Martin firmly believed that he needed lots of money to achieve his goal, so he locked in on the money as the only way to fulfill his desire. Since the money part wasn't working out very well so far, he therefore believed he was stuck and could not achieve his goal.

"Make your written goal about living on the estate, not about the money," I told him. "Make this about what you really want—the estate experience itself—not the money you think you need in order to have it."

When you focus on the thing you really want the money for, you will be more motivated and will make better decisions. Your goal will come to you much more quickly and easily because you're paying attention to the result you want instead of getting stalled by how to get there.

It was about two years later that I got a note in the mail from Martin.

In it, he told me he had recently received a phone call from a wealthy cousin who just happened to have a beautiful estate in New England. The cousin explained that he and his family were going abroad for two years, and he asked if Martin would be interested in acting as the caretaker of his estate while he was gone.

Would he like to be paid to live on a beautiful estate for two years?

Martin was writing to tell me that he now understood that the pursuit of money by itself was a dead end, and that once he got clear about the emotionally connected desire underneath his money-seeking, his treasured dream dropped right into his lap.

This is why I think it is so important for you to be very clear and strong about your deep desires—those things that make up the emotionally motivated "why" of your business. Don't get stuck on the money; stay focused on the underlying dream.

For example, the goal of "I want to make $10 million dollars" might become a deeper goal, such as, "I want to be free to work only when I want to." The desire for freedom in this case is the true emotional desire, and it will be much more powerful and motivating for this person in the long run than the money itself.

If you talk to a lot of people about this, as I do in my executive coaching, you will find that they have many emotional "whys" behind their drive for money.

Some people pursue money because they think it will give them social stature and respect.

Others have specific cherished goals they wish to reach, such as retiring, paying for a child's education, buying a home, or taking a trip.

Many people think that having more money will give them some safety in an uncertain world, that it will take away their fears and worries.

While it is true that having enough money for food, bills, and the other expenses of life reduces anxiety for most of us, once you start getting more money than that, it brings with it a brand-new set of anxieties. Don't believe me? Ask your friends who have lots of money.

You start worrying about losing it, about spending too much of it, about how to get more of it, about your tax rate, or about whether your investments are sound or safe. You find out that worry is free-floating and transferrable. Your past worries about not having enough money will morph into future worries about all the risks and responsibilities that come with having a lot of money.

So money is a complicated thing, and it flows in a transactional, psychological, and emotional world that is worth learning about so you can handle it right and have a chance of success with the business you will start.

After all, you want to have a happy, prosperous experience with your great idea.

Take action for traction: *How can you put the topic you just read into action?*

Think about *why* you will start your business as you work with these action items.

- When you open your own business, why will you do it? Write down all the reasons you can think of.

  _____

  _____

  _____

  _____

- Which of those reasons is the *most* important?

  _____

  _____

- Write down the biggest benefit of fulfilling your most important reason. What will change for the better in a big way for you and for others when it comes true?

  _____

  _____

How Your Beliefs About Money Make You Rich or Poor

Belief: An idea about something one accepts as true or real; a firmly held opinion or conviction —Google dictionary

If I were to ask fifty people on the street to share their beliefs about money, I would get a lot of different answers, and those answers would be all over the map. I know this because I have asked that question many times—to my clients and to audiences when I am presenting about business or money.

"Money is the root of all evil," someone will say.

"Money is freedom," someone else will say.

"You have to work really hard to make a lot of money" is a belief shared by a lot of people.

"Money is hard to get" and "You can't make much money without a college degree" are two widely held beliefs.

Each person who holds one of those beliefs assumes that his or her belief is true. People tend to believe that their own beliefs are the truth of the matter and that other people just don't quite get it.

Yet if we objectively examine beliefs themselves, we find varying degrees of inherent truth to them.

I know a lot of rich people, for instance, who don't work hard at all. Several of them call their brokers once or twice a week from their yachts or tennis clubs to change a few things with their portfolios, and that's their level of work.

So much for the belief that you have to work hard for your money.

We all know about people who have made lots of money despite the lack of a college degree—Richard Branson of Virgin Airlines, Bill Gates of Microsoft, Steve Jobs of Apple, Christy Walton of Walmart, and Michael Dell of Dell computers, to name a few.

So, money and degrees don't necessarily march together in lockstep, either.

"Money is hard to get" is a very interesting belief. People who look at it this way have usually worked hard or struggled to get their money, so they believe that their experience is "the way it is" about what it takes to make money.

They also may have other beliefs that support this one, such as "There's something wrong with money that comes easily, but if you work hard for it, it's okay" or "I have to earn whatever money I have."

Remember, America was founded by Puritans—a highly religious people whose belief that work is the Godly producer of all good things rolled on down through the years and still has great power in our culture today.

The truth is, if hard work were really what it takes to make lots of money, construction workers, coal miners, and roofers—those who work the hardest—would be the wealthiest people in the world.

Here's the thing about how your beliefs can keep you poor: you tend to think that your beliefs about money are absolutely true, which causes you to act in ways that reinforce those beliefs no matter what. In psychology, they call this tendency to act in ways that confirm our own viewpoints and beliefs "confirmation bias."

If, for example, you hold the belief that you must work hard for your money, you will make choices that confirm your belief. You will surround yourself with a life that rewards you for work and effort, and you will probably find it very hard to accept good things unless you feel you have earned them.

Another way your beliefs can hurt you and stop your success is when opposing beliefs collide.

Let's say you would like to have more money, maybe even a lot of money. Perhaps you believe it's a great thing to have a lot of money.

Let's say you also have a belief that rich people are jerks.

Since you definitely don't want to be a jerk, do you think you will ever let yourself become rich?

Since beliefs are the foundations of our actions, what do you think you would do in your work, and in your life, with this set of *conflicting* beliefs?

The answer is that you would end up acting out both of them in some way, even though they conflict.

Here's what that belief conflict I just mentioned might look like in action:

- You have a life that is interesting but without much money.

- You make a lot of money and then lose it, perhaps repeatedly.

- You seem to have a reverse Midas touch: you have a lot of opportunities, but they never amount to much, and you seem to repel money without knowing why.

- You do a lot of starting and stopping in your career. You can't quite seem to gain the ongoing momentum that would take you to prosperity.

Whatever you have going on in your inner belief system will very directly influence any business you might start. You can see why it might be a good idea to sort out your beliefs about money and work so they are not wrestling with each other unexamined while they pull your business down.

How You Can Change Beliefs That Are Stopping You

All of us have belief conflicts to some degree, and the first step in getting free is to question where they came from. Are they really your beliefs? How did you come to believe these things?

If you were to write down all your beliefs and ask yourself, "Where did I get each of these? Where did they come from?" you would probably see that a lot of them look pretty familiar. That's because they belonged to other people you have known before they belonged to you.

Where do you get your beliefs? Many of them come from your parents, your teachers, your friends, and all the other people you know. They also came from all the spoken and unspoken rules of the culture and society you grew up in.

You took on a mixture of those ideas and made them your own.

The first time I voted as a young man, I cast my ballot for the same people my parents voted for because I had absorbed my parents' beliefs about politics.

I very much wanted to be like my dad, so I voted the way he did at first, and I came into adulthood believing many of the things he did about people, about life, about how you should do things, and about how you should think.

You know how some people say that babies are blank slates when they are born, waiting to be written upon by life? That's not totally true, but it often works that way when it comes to beliefs. We tend to absorb the beliefs of people we feel close to because we want to be like them and feel close to them.

It was only after I learned much more about life and politics that I was able to challenge some of my previous unthinking opinions and beliefs about "how things are." Once I started doing that, I was free to either consciously adopt those opinions and beliefs or find other ones that suited me better.

Most people believe that you can change your life by changing your actions, and in fact you can do that to a certain extent. But if you don't change the beliefs that cause your actions, just changing the actions themselves will probably not be enough to create lasting change. For that, you need to change your beliefs.

Did you know that it is possible to change your beliefs? Having them now does not mean being stuck with them forever.

If you really want to change your life, change your beliefs. If you want to change your money life, change your money beliefs. Then you will naturally act according to the new, less limited beliefs that you select about money from that point forward. Your new beliefs, if you choose them well, will give you the platform inside of you to have what you want outside in the world, for your business, and for your life. What you want will line up with what you believe, and you can have it.

To begin the process of changing beliefs that hold you back, it is useful to see that beliefs are either limiting or unlimited; in other words, they either bind you or set you free.

Unlimited belief: I accept all the good in my life, and it can come to me from anywhere.

Limiting belief: I believe that the good in my life comes through my job and through my hard work.

The first belief opens all the doors and windows so good things can rain in on you. The second one allows for only one path to the good things in life—work.

If you really want all the success you desire in your business or in your life, you must first be certain that you have beliefs in place that will support that success.

Take action for traction: *How can you put the topic you just read about into action?*

Think about your beliefs about money as you work with these action items:

- What are your beliefs about money? Make a list of all of them—unlimited or limiting—and don't leave anything out. If you don't end up with somewhere between thirty and sixty beliefs on your list, you haven't dug deep enough yet.

    Examples of unlimited beliefs:
    "If I do what I love, the money will follow."

    "When it comes to my business, the sky is the limit."

    "There's nothing I can't do if I just keep at it."

    "Money comes whenever I need it."

    Examples of limiting beliefs:
    "Money is hard to come by."

    "It is not right to want a lot of money."

    "I need to have a large amount of money to live the life I want."

    "If I make too much money, I might lose my values and become somebody I won't like."

- Put a mark beside the beliefs on your list that you think might be holding you back from the success you want—the beliefs that feel limiting to you.

- Write down the opposite belief to each of your limiting beliefs as if it is true for you, in the present tense. Here are some examples.

    Limiting belief:
    "Money is hard to come by."

    Desired opposite belief:
    "Money comes easily to me."

    Limiting belief:
    "Money corrupts."

    Desired opposite belief:
    "I use money according to my strong ethical and moral standards."

When you write down the belief that you desire as if it is already true, you are telling yourself that you can claim it now.

We get more of what we focus upon, and this kind of "self-talk" brings you to focus upon unlimited beliefs that will support unlimited success for you and for any business you may own.

You will be successful inside and outside, and that kind of success survives the ups and downs.

Once you have developed a list of all your unlimited beliefs, sit quietly and write about them every now and then—whatever comes up. Affirm them with your writing, affirm that they are true for you, and they will take root in your thinking and your emotions.

If you wish to have a garden, you must gather good seeds, plant them in nutritious soil, and give them plenty of light and water. But the biggest ingredient of a successful garden is not the seeds, the soil, the sun, or the water. It is your attention and the regular cultivation you bring to it.

Without cultivation, a garden turns to weeds, and without cultivation, your beliefs squabble and contend with each other. This reduces your momentum to fits and starts in the areas of your life where those conflicts live.

Why Money Is Everything

Once you see that money is really about ideas, you can also begin to understand when you really need it and when you don't.

You don't need money to dream, think, talk, or make plans in your mind. You will, however, need a small or large amount of money to take your idea out into the world and build it as a business.

Money is to commerce as blood is to the human circulatory system. It allows all the people and organizations of the world to share what they have, back and forth, according to a mutually agreed-upon definition of value, which is symbolized most commonly by numbers, paper, or coins.

A journey is involved in moving from the founding idea of your business to the fact of having an operating business in the material world. You will navigate that distance with a need for money along the way that may be large or small, depending upon many factors.

A lot of entrepreneurs do not know in the beginning how to plan for the financing[18] of their businesses—they just begin. If they are very lucky, the business will finance itself, at least until it is established. But it is highly likely at some point that your business is going to need an infusion of cash to become what you want it to be.

---

[18] http://www.sba.gov/category/navigation-structure/starting-managing-business/starting-business/prepare-your-business-f-0

I have a wonderful client whom I shall call Richard. Richard is an extremely smart and determined person who started an amazing career in real estate by purchasing a single small house and renting it out. One house turned into many houses until Richard had a net worth of over a million dollars.

Now, you can already see that Richard needed some money for that first house—he had to buy it and pay for the repairs in preparation for bringing it on the rental market. He had to come up with a down payment, get a mortgage, purchase insurance, consult with a lawyer to draw up his company and rental documents, and advertise to find a tenant. All these things required money to arrange.

Richard is a very frugal person who did not have a lot of money left over from those expenses, so he managed his rental house using as little cash as possible since he wanted the house to pay for itself. He took none of its revenue for his own needs once he had a tenant, plowing the income from it into an account to cover unforeseen problems that might arise. He worked a day job to earn the money that supported his family.

Over time, the money in that income account grew, accumulating beyond necessary expenditures, and enough was left over for a down payment on another house, and then another. When he owned enough houses, there was enough money to put down on an apartment building.

At each step of the way, Richard had to come up with a loan to finance the purchase of new properties, but his business philosophy continued to be to operate those properties from the revenues they produced, with as little further borrowing and debt as possible. He used the cash flow produced by his properties to fund the down payments on new holdings and to cover his costs of doing business.

He also did not believe in keeping much cash on hand; he preferred to pay off debt whenever he had extra cash.

Many entrepreneurs want to start their businesses this way. They don't have much cash, so they want their businesses to be self-sufficient right away, and they want to minimize expenses and debt. They put their earnings back into their businesses and don't have much cash lying around.

But, as Richard found out, running on so little cash can get you in deep trouble.

A terrible recession came along, and all of a sudden the banks started behaving badly. They called in Richard's property loans early (yes, they can do that!), and their terms for the new loans that were crucial for his growth became outrageous and prohibitive.

All of his other loan payments and costs of business continued to demand regular payments, too, so Richard suddenly needed a lot of cash. Because he did not have back-up sources of credit or adequate cash reserves, his business nearly failed. It took him years to get back in the black and build up a good, solid cash reserve.

Entrepreneurs consistently underestimate the amount of money they will need to start and run their businesses and be profitable going forward. Undercapitalization[19] is one of the biggest reasons that new businesses fail, so in this sense, at this business stage, money is sometimes everything.

You can have all the good ideas in the world, but just know that you'll need at least *some* cash at various points to make those ideas real and keep them going, and it's always better to have more than enough available at all times than it is to underestimate your needs.

Once you give the green light to your great idea, be prepared to find the money you will need—in cash, loans, grants, gifts, or however you can get it—and always go for having more on hand than you think you will need.

There is a rule when you build a new home that you should be prepared to spend at least 25 percent more than you initially estimated for the project. I think that is a good rule as a minimum for starting a business, too. If you don't have extra money on hand to handle things you didn't think of or plan for, your peace of mind will vanish, and your business might even fail.

Nobody I know ever lost any sleep from having too much funding available for his or her business, but way too

---

[19] http://www.investopedia.com/terms/u/undercapitalization.asp

many people lose more than sleep because they don't have enough money when they need it.

Take action for traction: *How can you put the topic you just read about into action?*

Think about your sources of money as you work with this action item:

- A lot of good information and assistance is gathered together in one place about how to fund a business[20]: the Small Business Administration's website.

    Go to http://www.sba.gov/content/estimating-startup-costs, where you can work with estimates of how much money you will need if you choose to start that business you are thinking about.

---

[20] http://www.kiplinger.com/article/business/T049-C000-S001-5-ways-to-fund-your-small-business.html

So You Want to Be an Entrepreneur

Entrepreneur: A person who is willing to assume the responsibility, risks, and rewards of starting and operating a business.

Before you start building a business, let's start with a basic question.

Are you qualified to be an entrepreneur?[21]

When you interview for a job with a potential employer, that person evaluates you as to whether you are actually qualified for the job. You should probably do some self-examination in a similar way before you decide to launch your own business.

Are you qualified for this?

Here are some known qualities of successful entrepreneurs:

- Passionate about what they do
- Good at what they do
- Curious
- Able to live with some uncertainty
- Adaptable and creative with regard to change

---

[21] http://www.inc.com/eric-schurenberg/the-best-definition-of-entepreneurship.html

- Willing to take risks, but not impulsive, foolish risks
- Unwilling or unsuited to work for others
- Good at spotting and exploiting opportunities
- Persistent
- Patient and able to roll with the ups and downs
- Self-starting and self-directed
- In it for more than just the money — they usually have a strong vision of what they are working for
- Willing to fail and try again
- Most successful entrepreneurs are serial entrepreneurs, so persistence is also an important requirement.

None of us will have every one of these strengths, skills, and attributes to the highest degree, but it's good to know which ones you have and which ones you don't.

A note about strengths: please don't waste a lot of time and energy trying to learn to do things in areas in which you are not skilled or that you hate. That will just hang you up and slow you down. Find someone else to do those things — someone who is good at them and enjoys them, someone for whom they are strengths.

The biggest problem most entrepreneurs have is getting bogged down in a lot of stuff they are not suited for or stuff that is not within the boundaries of what their job should be. This is the entrepreneur's black hole!

Another thing you'll need to assess is your appetite for work because almost all entrepreneurs report feeling overworked. Part of that is because running a company is a complicated endeavor that requires a lot of attention, time, and effort, and part of it is the addictive, stressed-out belief that you have to be involved in everything or it will all fall apart.

You will need to guard against becoming a workaholic, which is a very common affliction for small business entrepreneurs. Your goal from the very beginning must be to figure out how to do only the things that you *should* do (your job description) and give the rest away to others who are good at those tasks.

The definition of your job will continually change as you and your company both grow, so that job description will never stop evolving.

There is a story about this—the story of the empty plate.

I have a friend, John, a physicist and engineer who worked at high levels in several major corporations. During his first day at his new position as a senior vice president, he was sent to meet with an experienced vice president who would be his mentor.

This mentor said to John, "The biggest thing you have to remember about this job is that it's not about putting more things on your plate, it is about keeping everything off your plate except for the things that are directly your responsibilities. At this level, everyone wants a piece of you, and you will quickly be overwhelmed if you don't follow this one piece of advice. If you allow others to put things on your plate that don't belong there, you will have no room left for the things that you must do, the things that are essential to your job description."

THE EMPTY PLATE PRINCIPLE

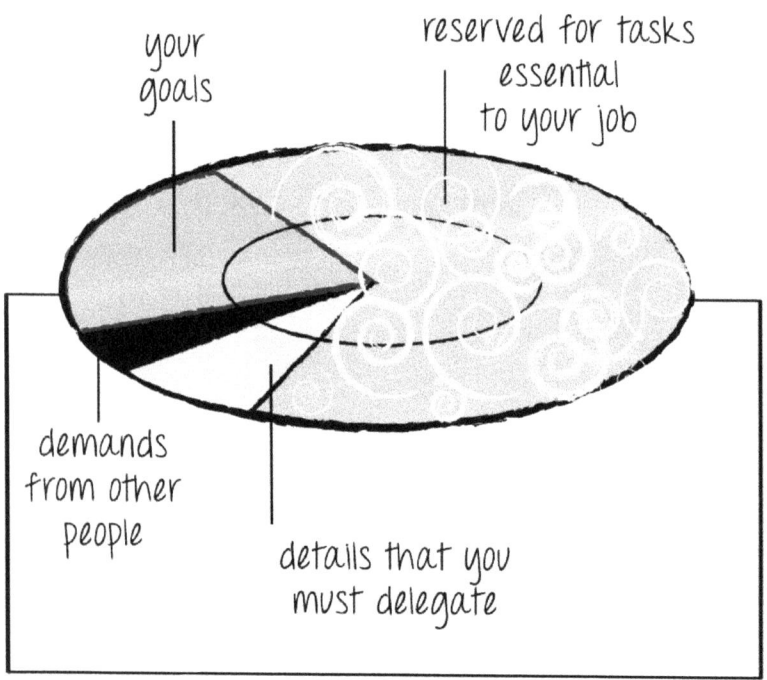

This advice was given to a senior vice president in a major corporation, and it also holds true for you, wherever you are in your experience, business size, or responsibility level. It is extremely hard to do in practice, though, because every day offers a constant parade of temptations to load up your plate with things that don't belong there.

To make this disciplined approach work, you have to be able to say no.[22] You have to have boundaries with people, time, and tasks. If you don't, this entrepreneur thing won't be any fun at all.

Now, having said all that, you may not have the money or the people at various times in the beginning to do the things you shouldn't be doing—that's going to happen. The trick will be to do those things only temporarily and not get married to them over time.

It is very difficult to do this in actual practice because taking on something new is so much easier than letting go of it later when you should and trusting that someone else will handle it well.

Not only must you be able to let go when needed, but you will also have to become comfortable with ongoing uncertainty and change. Unless you are buying a franchise, there is usually not much of a roadmap for entrepreneurs at the beginning. No matter how much you prepare—and I hope it's a lot—you will still, at times, be making this up as you go along, making decisions and recalibrating your

---

[22] http://www.businessinsider.com/this-is-how-successful-people-say-no-2014-8

course without as much certainty about the outcome as you might like. In everything from your plans to your finances, constant change will keep you on your toes.

It helps in those times to have had some experience as a poker player. Poker[23] requires that you play the game and make important decisions based on very little information about what everybody else is doing.

Whether or not you are a good poker player, you will, of course, have the advantage of starting your business with a business plan.[24] If you don't, you might just as well take out all your seed money and set it on fire. You will have more fun that way, and you won't suffer as much. With a business plan, you know what you have and where you are going, at least in the beginning.

---

[23] http://www.pokerlistings.com/poker-rules
[24] https://www.sba.gov/writing-business-plan

Just Plan Confusing

Many kinds of plans will help your business over time, but the most important one in the beginning is your *business plan*. A *business* plan is often confused with a *strategic* plan, so let's get our definitions straight to start with.

A business plan is a written document that describes your proposed business, its objectives, its initial strategies, the market in which it operates, and its initial financial forecasts. It is a data-rich and hope-filled map for the very beginning of your business. It is the "what my business will be in the beginning" plan to get you started.

If you are lining up funding through a financial organization, they will request a completed business plan to use as part of their decision-making process for your loan.

You will need a *strategic plan* after your business has been up and running for a while. This is a map of *how* your business will get where you want it to be in the future, and it is full of specific goals and plans to get you there.

Why do you absolutely need both of these plans? As one of my teachers once said, "If you don't know where you're going, you'll never get there."

Take action for traction: *How can you put the topic you just read about into action?*

Think about what you would need for a possible business as you work with these action items:

- Go to this page at the Small Business Administration: http://www.sba.gov/category/navigation-structure/starting-managing-business/starting-business/how-write-business-plan.

    Read all the short articles there about how to put together the various parts of a business plan, just so you know what's involved if you decide to move forward with starting your business.

- Make a list of the things you would need in order to complete the plan, and another list of the resources you would require for the business itself. Then the lists of everything you need will be right in front of you so you can look at them. These things are the nuts and bolts of your business in the beginning. By doing this exercise, most people get a pretty good feel for what putting their business idea into action would look like. You need to know what it looks like so you can make good plans and a strong start in your business.

Getting Rid of the Boss? Not So Fast

If you ask most entrepreneurs why they started their own businesses, they would say it was so they could have the independence and freedom to do what they want and to have control over their work and their lives.

What actually happens when they take the plunge is often quite different.

They thought they were getting rid of their bosses, only to find out that they have signed on to having all kinds of different bosses in their self-employment.

I'm defining "boss" as any person or people who have control over what you do in your work.

So instead of having just one boss, you end up with customers, employees, vendors, regulators, taxing entities, and attorneys, to name a few, all of whom have their own demands and authority over you. They have authority because they have the power to determine how your business can operate and whether or not it can succeed.

So sure, get rid of that bad old boss. Just realize that the new boss is going to wear a lot of faces, and all those people you will be accountable to will make things a whole lot more complicated.

This isn't to say that the whole self-employment[25] thing isn't worth it; most business owners would tell you it is. The freedom you get is just a different kind of freedom than you imagined it would be before you tried it.

So if you think you're getting into your business to fly free as a bird, unfettered by all those unreasonable people and their unending demands where you used to work, think again.

If the thought of all this puts a knot in your stomach and makes you yearn to run back to the security of a job working for someone else, that's normal.

But remember, there is no real security anymore in working for someone else. The old days of spending your life with one company, getting a pension, retiring, and not working anymore—those days are gone.

People in America today can expect to have between ten and fifteen jobs over the course of their working years. This means they will do a whole lot of shifting of positions or careers, which in essence puts them in the business of managing and promoting their own career track at numerous times. This looks, in many ways, like self-employment—you are responsible for you, whether or not you work for someone else. The belief that there is safety in being employed by someone else is increasingly an illusion.

---

[25] http://www.forbes.com/sites/glassheel/2012/04/12/13-signs-you-are-meant-to-be-self-employed/

The question, then, is which self-employment track are you better suited for? Do you like periods of being embedded in organizations, then moving to another organization or career path? Or do you prefer to just be on your own all the way, ready for all the risks and rewards that come with that decision?

Entrepreneurship is not for everyone, and there is no failure in knowing it's not for you, but it works out best if you go into it with your eyes open, having chosen it for what it is, with skills, attitudes, and emotions that will help you succeed and enjoy it.

Don't waste your time, money, and energy if it really isn't for you. Reluctant, toe-in-the-water entrepreneurs really suffer, and things don't usually end well.

But if you are one of those people who are just twitching to stop working for someone else and start working for yourself, let's go. Let's talk about how you can do that.

Take action for traction: *How can you put the topic you just read about into action?*

Think about the pluses and minuses of both staying employed and starting a business as you work with these action items:

- What things do you like about your job and being employed? Make a list of the things that are great about having that job, or any job.

- Make another list of all the advantages of being an entrepreneur and owning your own business. Why does it make great sense to you to do that?

- What kinds of feelings and reactions did you have while you made the two lists? Write down your reactions for each of those options and how they made you feel in your gut. If words or phrases came to you while making the lists, write those down, too.

The two lists you created, along with your feelings and reactions while making them, are your internal "weather report" about how you are feeling right now with regard to employment and self-employment.

There are a lot of things to learn, know, and do that will give your business its best chance to succeed. If you are willing to take your time, gather your resources, and prepare well before you actually open for business, you will have a much better chance to survive and thrive than if you just jump into it.

Think of your business-to-be as a boat; you need to make sure it is really seaworthy before you take it out into the big waves and wind.

The Bureau of Labor Statistics[26] says that 66 percent of new businesses are still in existence two years after their birth, and 44 percent are still in existence four years after. Looking at the other side of those numbers, that means 34 percent don't make it through the first two years, and 56

---

[26] http://www.bls.gov/ces/

percent of new businesses don't make it through the first four years.

And how many of those surviving businesses do you think are actually robust and successful, with happy owners? That's different than "survival," and the number is pretty small.

I believe that the biggest single factor in the high percentage of new business failures, as well as the inability to thrive for many surviving new businesses, is that their owners did not properly prepare and plan for success—they just jumped in.

"Woo-hoo! I've got a great idea, let's go!"

If you can instead say, "I've got a great idea, so let's look at it, prepare for it, and test it until it's really ready," you can be one of the few entrepreneurs who does not have to go crazy trying to survive numerous challenges that were self-inflicted, predictable, and avoidable.

Falling in Love with Your Big Idea

That all makes sense, doesn't it? Prepare and plan thoroughly for success? It would obviously help the start-up survival rate, so why don't more people do it?

The culprit is love.

Many people don't prepare well because they fall in love with their big idea.

Common sense and detailed, thorough preparation are very hard to stick with when you fall in love; you start acting just as you do when you fall in love with a person!

When we are falling in love with a person, we are told that we should take it slow, wait, and be sure about the person before we have sex and get committed.

That does not happen very often either, does it?

The good intentions usually melt like snowflakes in the furnace of infatuation, high-flying expectations, and raging hormones.

Which is all proof that emotions can take over our minds!

The same thing happens with a business idea. We even go through the same psychological and emotional stages of falling in love:

- Attraction: Wow! What a great idea!

- Fixation: I think about it all the time and have a lot of fantasies about what it would be like to have it!

- Yearning: Past disappointments and burdens with work cause me to yearn deeply for something new.

- Falling in love: This is what I want to do! Yes! It's so perfect!

- Decision to do it: I'm going to go for it!

- Over-commitment: I want it now!

The bulldozer of emotion and desire often runs right over all the thinking and preparation, and people jump into their new business just as they jumped into the arms of their first sweetheart at age sixteen, even when they have more sensible intentions.

Now, I'm not saying you don't need emotion and desire to be part of your process when you develop your idea and as you perform your ongoing work.

Au contraire, you need your head, your heart, and your hands to put it all together so your business comes alive and stands out. It's just that you also need to be able to resist the seduction of your emotions when they want you to take action for its own intoxicating sake. You must be able to stay with your ability to make good, wise decisions even when you're feeling a lot of emotions pulling you this way and that.

The best way to begin to do this is to observe that you have two parts inside of you that are both trying to run the show.

One part of you is falling in love with your ideas and riding an emotional roller-coaster[27] up and down as your mind goes ninety miles a minute and impulses to act, act, act continuously sweep over you. At the same time, another part of you is a thoughtful, rational, and sensible person who is advocating that you take your time and do things right.

The key is to be aware of which part is running the show at any given time.

---

[27] http://www.brainyquote.com/quotes/keywords/roller_coaster.html

When you know that, you can encourage the thoughtful processes and hold off from acting on the impulses until you prove them out. Or, if you are a person who overthinks things, you might consider allowing yourself to get out of your head now and then and really feel what's going on. For most people, though, it's the emotional part of you at this stage of things that is always ready to take over the show.

A good way to bring focus to your mind at this time is to give your brain process tasks to do that don't require big decisions or changes. This will help you conceptualize and explore your business idea in a linear, thinking way, and will give some balance to the side of you that wants to just charge ahead. The human mind loves tasks, and your emotions will be less likely to jerk you around if you are following an agenda and getting something appropriate done.

Take action for traction: *How can you put the topic you just read about into action?*

Think about how you tend to react to exciting, new things as you work with these action items:

- When something new and exciting comes along, how do you tend to respond?

    _____

    _____

- A good example of this is:

  _____
  _____
  _____
  _____

- When you respond that way, how do you usually feel?

  _____
  _____
  _____
  _____

- If you were to respond differently when something new and exciting came along, what would you do instead?

  _____
  _____
  _____
  _____

The *Business* Part of Owning a Business

Before you decide to actually start working on your business idea, there is a key question you need to ask yourself: am I willing to learn whatever it is that I don't know about running a business so my big idea will have a chance of making it out there in the world?

I have seen many entrepreneurs who love the service or product their big idea is centered around but who don't have any attraction or taste for the business part of things. I recall one person who opened the clothing store of her dreams without any retail experience and without any specific knowledge about the retail clothing industry.

Then there was a restaurant owner who loved to cook but got lost in all the details of running the restaurant and ended up hating her business because that side of things swallowed up her cooking time.

Most entrepreneurs are drawn to making a business out of something they love to do, and that's a good thing.

Being passionate about what you bring to the world is a key factor in lasting success. But if you have no appetite for learning all you need to know about the *business* end of things—the critical processes necessary to connect what you offer with the people who will need and buy it—you have two options:

1. Find other people to do the business part of the work so you can keep doing just the part you love. You might take on a partner, for example, whose entire focus and skill set is business management. Even if you do this, though, you will still need to know enough about business to monitor the other people involved to make sure they are doing their jobs right. There are many horror stories out there about what happens when creative people get too disconnected from the commercial side of their companies.

2. If you don't want to do that, you probably need to do what you love as a hobby instead of trying to turn it into a business.

   A fair number of people who have had established businesses based on something they were passionate about will tell you that trying to bring that passion out into the business world killed it dead. They really enjoyed doing the part they loved, but turning it into a job that they had to work at every day made it lose its sparkle.

So there is no foul and no harm if you do what you love in a noncommercial way. All your friends telling you that you are a great baker does not constitute enough of a reason in itself for you to open a bakery.

You need to be passionate[28] about what you do, and you should also feel genuinely interested and open about learning the business piece, too, if you want to take your passion successfully beyond being a well-loved hobby.

The most successful entrepreneurs know that they must be completely willing to learn about business and to do whatever it takes to turn their ideas into sales.

In this context, I define "business" as all the applied knowledge, skills, and practices that are needed to successfully prepare and sell products and services in the marketplace.

Here is a partial list of some of the business functions you might need in your company in order to turn your idea into a successful business:

- Product / service research, development, updating, and design
- Manufacturing
- Purchasing
- Supply chain management
- Market development
- Sales
- Customer service

---

[28] http://www.linkedin.com/today/post/article/20130704005710-7374576-finding-your-passion-in-work-20-awesome-quotes

- Inventory and shipping
- Quality assurance
- Administrative tasks
- Human resources (hiring, firing, and supervision of others)
- Finance (loans, payroll, taxes, and accounts)
- Regulation compliance, licenses, and insurance
- Internet technology (IT)

In the beginning, it may be just you who wears all the business hats. This is often a necessary but dangerous state of affairs that is common to the entrepreneur start-up process.

It is necessary because you may not initially have enough money or other resources to bring on everyone and everything you might like to have. It is dangerous because entrepreneurs who start this way often find out later that they have acquired an almost unbreakable habit of trying to micromanage everything about their businesses, sticking their fingers into everything even when it has grown to the point where they are overwhelmed and should absolutely be letting other people take on parts of it.

This gets in the way of growing their businesses big-time.

So there you would be, with all the business responsibilities and decisions that starting and running a business bring, wearing all those hats. Unless you really know something about operating the key areas of your business that are necessary for its success, your enthusiasm and personal leadership alone will not be enough to make a go of it.

It is, of course, unreasonable to think that any one person would be able to know and perform all the functions of a business really well. That is why, to avoid cementing yourself into that deadly, overwhelming micromanagement habit, it is a good idea to allow other people to take on even small parts of your business functions as soon as you can.

If you can't hire someone initially, to answer the phones for example, and you do your own administrative work, technology can help with that. I use a phone system that gives me all the features of a robust answering system for a very small monthly fee and sends my messages to all my mobile devices so I am connected to my business whenever and wherever I want to be.

Virtual assistants—real people with real administrative skills—can do a lot of your administrative work at their own locations for a fraction of what it would cost you to hire an actual administrative assistant to come to your office every day.

Today's lean business model has only as many people as are really needed to perform the core functions of a business as in-house employees, and it gives everything else over to automation, outside contractors, and strategic partners. This can save a whole lot of time, energy, and money as you are scrambling to get your business off the ground and as you grow.

As an example, it has been many, many years since automakers designed and manufactured every part for their cars in their own plants. They have long known the economies of scale and cash savings that come about through hiring outside experts to do the things they really don't have to do themselves.

So a good rule of thumb is to contract out[29] anything you don't really have to do and anything that would slow you down or distract you from your core mission. Hire only the people you need for that and keep your own job description[30] very focused.

The specifics of your core mission, and of your personal job description, should be included in your initial business plan so you will have something to measure your own work by day-to-day.

If you try to do everything yourself, without the help you need, you will concoct a certain recipe for burnout and eventual failure. At the very least, running your business won't be much fun.

---

[29] http://www.irs.gov/Businesses/Small-Businesses-&-Self-Employed/Independent-Contractor-Defined
[30] http://www.businessdictionary.com/definition/job-description.html

However, there is one area in which you should definitely be cautious about involving other people in your business—taking on a business partner.

The Mixed Blessings of Business Partnerships

Business partnership: a business or firm owned and run by two or more partners.

Strategic partnership: an agreement with another person or company to undertake business endeavors together on each other's behalf while still maintaining separate business structures and interests. This can involve financing, sales, marketing, distribution, or other activities that are defined by the partners.

When you consider starting a business, you might be thinking about whether to do it alone or take on a business partner to own and operate part of the business with you.

You'll need to think about this very carefully.

Partnerships can sometimes work wonders for a business, but if they go wrong, things could go very badly for you as well as for your company.

Here are some of the common benefits that partnership can bring to your business:

- *The business will do better.* Food businesses, for instance, are often family businesses in which family members also function as business partners. Family members cover the essential company roles in a unified, all-on-the-same-page way, their skills complement each other, and turnover in critical positions is low.

- *Someone else has the money, access, connections, or expertise that you don't have* that is crucial to the business. That person brings enough value to the company to make it worthwhile to give him or her a piece of the ownership.

- *Someone who works for you is so valuable* to your business that elevating that person to the status of partner secures a deeper level of participation and commitment from him or her.

- *Partnership provides moral support,* brainstorming, and shared decision-making—you're not in this alone.

- *A partner brings a set of complementary strengths* in areas where you may be weak or need to grow.

- *You have backup.*

When partnerships work out well, those benefits are wonderful, and the company prospers in ways it could not without the contributions of all the partners.

Some examples of great partnerships:

Thomas Edison, J. P. Morgan, and the Vanderbilt family:
Thomas Edison, like many entrepreneurs, had more good ideas than money. He linked up with a group of wealthy investors, including the financier J. P. Morgan and the Vanderbilt family. His financial partners contributed the cash that allowed him to advance from perfecting the light bulb to building a network of 121 Edison central power stations across America.

Sam, Jack, Albert, and Harry Warner:
The Warner brothers founded what would later become Warner Brothers Studios. The sons of Polish immigrants, they revolutionized the movie business when Sam Warner obtained the technology that allowed them to make "talkies," movies with sound. That innovation killed the silent film era, and the brothers went on to build Warner Brothers into one of the all-time top movie studios.

Joan Ganz Cooney and Jim Henson of Sesame Street:
Most people think Jim Henson invented *Sesame Street*, but Joan Ganz Cooney founded the Children's Television Network and *Sesame Street*.

She spotted Henson and his puppets and knew they would fit in with her children's program, but Henson was initially uninterested because he was working on his own projects that were more oriented toward adults.

Joan Cooney persisted and finally convinced Jim Henson to bring his Muppets to her *Sesame Street* program, and the rest is super-successful history.

Richard and Maurice McDonald:
Ray Croc was the well-known owner of fast-food giant McDonalds, but he was not the founder.

Richard and Maurice McDonald were the first burger shop owners to set up a kitchen as a mechanized assembly line and turn out fast food the way we know it today. They had already sold 21 McDonald's franchises when Ray Croc, who was then a paper cup salesman from Illinois, discovered them and bought their business.

Coco Chanel and Pierre Wertheimer:
The story of Coco and Pierre is a cautionary tale about how bad it can get when a partnership doesn't work out well.

Coco Chanel created her iconic Chanel No. 5 perfume and, two years later, teamed up with successful businessman Pierre Wertheimer to help her establish and grow her company, *Parfums Chanel*. Chanel had the name and the fame, but Wertheimer had the money, connections, and marketing savvy she needed and lacked.

Sadly, she accepted only a 10 percent share of the company as her portion of the partnership, with Wertheimer taking most of the rest. Although this made her a wealthy woman, she contested their financial arrangement in later years but failed to get it changed. Today the Wertheimer family owns 100 percent of the company.

This leads us to the fact that partnerships have some common drawbacks as well:

- Partnerships are relationship-based, and relationships are not easy. If the relationship goes bad, it can take the business with it.

- You may find out that your partner is lazy, incompetent, unreliable, or untrustworthy. All these things come down to one partner not pulling a fair share of the load and thus putting your business in jeopardy.

- Partnerships are easy to form and not so easy to end. That's why you need a written partnership agreement.

- Since decisions must be made together, disagreements are bound to occur. If they are not handled well, they can hurt your company.

- Your partner is not your employee, and you must be able to collaborate instead of giving orders. If you are not skilled at collaboration, this can be a problem.

- Profits are shared, and determining each partner's value can be tricky. Resentments about money are common between partners.

- Most partnerships have unlimited liability, which means that either of you—and both of you—are responsible for all of the company's commitments, errors, and debts.

The most damaging, troublemaking mistake I see so many partners make is not drawing up a comprehensive partnership agreement[31] with the input of an attorney when they first join up. This type of agreement protects both the partners and the business and prevents a lot of trouble down the line.

---

[31] https://www.sbdc.duq.edu/Files/Admin/Webnotes/1SamplePartnershipAgreement.pdf

Some of the areas covered by such an agreement would define what happens to your company if any co-owner:

- Wants to leave or dissolve the business
- Wants to retire
- Dies
- Goes through personal bankruptcy
- Wants to sell his or her shares to someone else
- Gets a divorce
- Stops performing the duties of his or her partnership satisfactorily

I remember all too many partnerships in which something that happened to one partner strongly troubled the others or threatened the company. In those cases, there were absolutely no agreements in place to help with any of it. The time for such agreements to be made is in the beginning of the partnership, not when trouble has already found you.

I recall the advertising company with three partners, one of whom was the managing partner. The trouble in this case came from the fact that the partners had no agreement about what the managing partner could or could not do in that role, so the business almost ground to a halt because of the constant conflicts that erupted when the managing partner tried to manage.

There was the musical instrument company—a family-owned business—in which the father was the president, his wife was the accountant, one child was the sales director, and the other child was the production manager.

There were no written job descriptions, compensation plans[32], organizational charts[33], or succession plans[34] for any of those positions or people. Common business structures and practices were ignored.

The business of the company was severely affected by the constant backstabbing and fighting among family members due to the lack of agreements about how the business should be run, who should do what, and who should get or not get resources, favored status, and compensation.

One thing was very clear—they all got a tremendous amount of aggravation and stress from their lack of clarity.

---

[32] http://www.wikihow.com/Develop-a-Compensation-Plan
[33] https://www.google.com/search?q=organizational+chart&sa=X&espv=210&es_sm=119&tbm=isch&tbo=u&source=univ&ei=ldI-U_bMCYfgsASmlYKQAw&ved=0CD0QsAQ&biw=1600&bih=734
[34] http://www.investopedia.com/articles/pf/07/succession_planning.asp

Why Partnering with Family and Friends Can Be Trouble

It might seem, on the face of it, that partnering with a friend or relative is a good idea. After all, you know each other well, and your bonds are strong. You would have someone familiar to help you steer your business where it should go.

When it works, this can be true, but the failure rate for partnerships with close people far exceeds the failure rate for partnerships that are only business based.

There is a reason for that, and it is because you have stepped into the world of dual roles. When you have more than one type of relationship with the same person, those relationship roles can conflict at times and exert uneven influences upon your thinking and actions.

She is a friend who also works in your business. *He* is an employee who becomes your friend. *They* are members of your family and your family business, and they are supposed to just focus on your business relationship while at work and leave all the other stuff that's in your personal relationship at the door.

Right.

It is almost impossible for anyone in a dual relationship to successfully juggle the different situations and demands of each role and keep both relationships separate and clear. Situations at work will conflict with the realities of the personal relationship at some point, and both relationships can suffer as a result.

Even if a partnership is contractual in nature instead of being a full business ownership partnership, the same problems can arise.

I remember a businesswoman—a company owner—who hired a consultant. They worked very well together, and their work synergy was so good over time that they became friends.

They started mingling business and friendship activities.

Outside the office, they got together for lunches and invited each other to parties. They shared very personal information with each other in long talks, and they hiked and went to concerts and just hung out.

Then one day the business relationship smacked right up against the friendship.

The consultant had been hired to evaluate the owner's business and to make recommendations to her about solutions to some very tough problems she was having.

When you are a consultant, you must be able to tell your client the truth about what you see and what you recommend at all times. That is what the client is paying you for!

In this case, the consultant had to tell his client (now also his friend) a very difficult truth—her business wasn't going to work the way she was conducting it, and major changes would be needed in order for it to succeed. Those changes would be disruptive and costly, and would go against what he knew she wanted to do.

She had invested heavily in her current business with both her time and money, and she really didn't want to hear that she had to make fundamental changes. She did not want to hear what he had to say.

When he gave her his recommendations, she felt betrayed because this person who was her friend was now causing her pain at work.

A new kind of immediate and ongoing tension set in between them as discussions about this critical matter proceeded.

Suddenly it felt very awkward to be friends.

The business owner was angry with him about her business, and he was tense and defensive with her because he felt he had obligations to her that went beyond the business, so he couldn't figure out moment to moment whether to be friendly or businesslike.

Ultimately, she ended his consulting contract, and they withdrew from each other and stopped interacting as friends.

The business tensions overcame the friendship. It was a classic case of dual roles and a double loss for both of them—a great relationship at work and a great relationship as friends.

It is much cleaner and easier to manage one type of relationship with the close people in your life and another type of relationship with the businesspeople in your life than it is to combine them. The odds of successfully managing a dual relationship are very low over time.

Here are some other recommendations for you to reflect on when you think you need a partner:

1. Whenever possible, hire people to do what you need done instead of giving away part of your company for it. Look at all the things you think you need a partner for, and see if there are other ways you can get them done. Once you give away any part of your business, it is very difficult and often very expensive to get it back.

2. Don't be partners with your relatives or friends, and don't hire them, either.

3. Use consultants[35], executive coaches[36], or mentors[37], or take classes, for the learning, assistance, and support you need to manage and grow your business. You can get a great deal of what you

---

[35] http://www.businessnewsdaily.com/4610-business-consultant.html
[36] http://hbswk.hbs.edu/archive/4853.html
[37] http://www.forbes.com/sites/martinzwilling/2012/03/20/effective-business-mentoring-is-a-relationship/

need from people who will teach it to you in a contract role instead of a partnership role. Contracting is cheaper in a whole lot of ways, and it is easier to avoid dual roles that way.

4. If you decide to bring on a partner, hire an attorney you both trust and have a detailed partnership agreement drawn up that protects both of you. Do not deepen any business you might already be doing together or make new commitments with each other until this agreement is completed and signed.

5. Create a trial period to begin the partnership— 90 days, six months, whatever amount of time would give you a really good idea of what it's like to work so closely with this person in your business. Pay your auditioning partner well for this time, and set things up to give either of you an easy out at any point during the trial period.

6. You can also build a compensation plan and ownership shares package for your new partner that will increase in steps after a successful trial period instead of sharing all profits at the highest level right away. Tie those compensation increases to measurable benchmarks—specifically defined accomplishments that demonstrate the growing success of the partnership. You can decide together ahead of time what those measuring points will look like and what the ownership shares and compensation increases will be.

7. When conflicts come up, resolve them quickly or get some help to do so. Don't let them fester. Anybody can have a relationship honeymoon in the beginning of a venture when everything goes smoothly, but how you handle conflicts when they come up will really define how the partnership will go.

8. If, at any point, it becomes clear that it is not going to work out for either of you to be partners anymore, let the partnership go so you can move on to greater success.

As you can see, full business partnership is a big step that needs to be taken carefully, if at all. Getting into strategic partnerships, on the other hand, is one of the smartest things you can do for your business.

Take action for traction: *How can you put the topic you just read about into action?*

Consider how you would feel about taking on a partner for your new business as you work with these action items:

- Where are you on a scale of 1–10 about starting a business with a partner? If the number that comes to you is less than eight, it's probably not a good idea for you to have a partner, and you can go on to read below about having strategic partners instead.

- If your number was eight or above and a partner might still make sense, who do you think might be good partner material for you? Is there more than one person? Might you have more than one partner? Write down the names of any partner candidates.

- After you have the name(s), write down all the good things that having that person as a partner could do for you. How would you and your business benefit from the partnership?

- Also write down any possible reasons not to choose that person or people—any hesitations you might have about them.

Doug Hickok

Strategic Partners Are Money in the Bank

Strategic partnership: an agreement between individuals or companies to undertake business endeavors individually or together on each other's behalf while still maintaining separate business structures and interests. This can involve financing, sales, marketing, distribution, delivery of services, or other activities, as defined by the partners.

Starbucks is a good example of a company that actively seeks out strategic partnerships to its great advantage. In 1993, the company entered into an agreement with Barnes and Noble bookstores to provide cafe services in their stores—a partnership that turned out well for both companies.

Starbucks went on to create strong alliances with United Airlines, Kraft Foods, and the NAACP. In the case of the NAACP, the two organizations share many goals and values about social and economic justice. Strategic partnerships aren't always just about business. You can have a strategic partner for anything you want to do in life.

Subway sandwich stores are now everywhere, including those that are embedded in other businesses as well as freestanding ones. They partner with Walmart, gas stations, and strip malls, gaining new customers for themselves and bringing lively foot traffic to the businesses that host them.

On a smaller scale, my friend Brandon is an insurance agent who does not just wait for the phone to ring when it comes to bringing in new customers. Brandon has strategic partnerships with many people who generate a steady stream of referrals for him. He has arrangements, for instance, with auto glass shops, where he sends his insurance customers with broken windows, and the auto glass companies send him people who need better auto insurance. Back and forth it goes.

Doctors routinely thrive in a web of strategic alliances. They affiliate with hospitals, which often supply them with discounted office space, expensive new technologies, and a steady flow of patients. The doctors reciprocate by bringing new patients, income, and expertise to the hospitals. They also develop reciprocal referrals with other physicians and health-care service providers.

You probably recall a time when you were in a doctor's office and the doc pulled out another doc's card to refer you out for something you needed. That referral card at the ready was a sign of an ongoing strategic partnership.

A strategic partnership gives you the benefit of someone pulling out your card and sending people to you who are already primed to buy what you sell. At their best, strategic partners can help you build your business much faster than you could alone. They can really help your business without the entanglements of a full business partnership or the costs of an expanded sales force.

Here's what it takes to make a strategic partnership work well:

- The benefits must go both ways. One-way referrals do not constitute a partnership.

- The people on both sides of the agreement work hard to keep sending a steady stream of referrals to each other so the benefits are consistent over time. Unequal effort will unbalance the partnership.

- The efforts and investments required of both parties in the partnership are fair and well defined.

- The return on your investment of time, effort, and everything else involved is big enough to justify doing it.

As with full business partnerships, it is always a good idea to have the core agreements you make written down, although sometimes these strategic alignments of business interests are so loose that this feels unnecessary.

The risks of having bad outcomes because of dual relationships still exist in any type of partnership, so the closer you are personally to your strategic partners, the more dual-role risks there are.

Any dual-role relationship anywhere in your life will tend to be layered and somewhat difficult because it is more complex and demands more conscious management of the different roles involved. The image that comes to my mind is of a person driving two horses around a track while standing up, with one foot on each horse. You can do it, but it's not easy.

Take action for traction: *How can you put the topic you just read about into action?*

Think about who might make good strategic partners for you as you work with these action items:

- What professions or businesses are natural fits to refer their customers to the business you are considering? Could you easily refer back to them? Write down the names of some people who might fit in this mutual referral loop with you.

- Are there other ways besides referrals that strategic partners could help you? Someone puts your product in her stores, or you join together for trade shows, or you make presentations to certain types of potential customers together. Write them down.

How Do You Know That Your Great Idea Will Work?

Before you can know the clear answer to that question, you need to do some real thinking and exploring about a lot of other stuff.

Start by sitting down in front of your computer and making a list of exactly what it is you would be selling to your customers. Is it a product, a service, or a combination of both? List all the products and services you have in mind and all the ways you might offer them for sale to your customers.

You might be thinking of opening an Internet technology business, for instance. When you make a list all of the Internet technology services you think you would like to offer, it might be quite a list: selling and fixing computers, building websites, search engine optimization, creating business Intranet networks, selling file storage space in the cloud, or selling accessory hardware.

It is great to be able to provide all of these things, but this is also where a lot of business owners make a big mistake.

They look at their list and decide they are going to market the entire list of services as a menu. "We can do some of this or some of that, whatever you choose."

The business owner thinks he or she is doing customers a favor by offering everything in a menu, but that isn't how potential customers want to find what they need. They go to the Internet to eliminate menus and to get right to the point of what they want. They can find a search engine expert, or a computer repair shop, or a cloud computing space offer simply by Googling that specific thing. They don't have to wade through a menu to find it.

Menus in any form are the equivalent of phone trees, those endless phone menu choices we have to make when we call a business before we get to speak to someone. We all hate phone trees, and many of us hate menus, so we instinctively look first for people who are experts at the one thing we need to have done, and on Google, the single-service experts stand out.

So don't offer a menu—specialize in something.

Cafeterias, with their big menus and huge variety of food, used to be really big in America. There used to be cafeterias in every town, and they were quite successful.

Not anymore.

It's harder to find a cafeteria these days because other restaurant owners have done such a good job of specializing, and Americans no longer have to go to a one-size-fits-all restaurant and figure out which part of the menu they like.

Doug Hickok

There are still specialty buffet restaurants for people who want to expand on the main choice and for people who think the variety is fun. But more and more, we choose a restaurant based upon the particular type or style of food that is sold there. We have become specialists in our food tastes as well as in all our other tastes.

Say to a friend that you are hungry, and nine times out of ten, that friend will ask, "What kind of food are you hungry for?"

We can go get some Italian, Mexican, Ethiopian, seafood, Japanese, Chinese, salad, chicken, or barbecue—the list is endless. Today's consumers treat food selection just like any other choice on Google, which is to say, they can find exactly what they want and leave all the other options behind! They have become more sophisticated in their food tastes, they have technology, and they are no longer attracted to menus that require them to make a lot of choices among food types and presentations.

As consumers, we tend to stick with our choices once we make them. It's hard to open our minds to trying something new when we already know something we like.

We also tend to like small choices better than big ones, and single choices rather than multiple ones. Nature wired us with those tendencies, and they have been accentuated because the pace of life these days has become so incredibly fast, and we are asked to make so many choices every day that we are relieved when we are presented with simpler decisions to make.

Choosing the specialty option for your business simplifies customers' lives and makes it easier for them to buy, so if you are a businessperson who specializes, that is a very good trend for your bottom line.

Doug Hickok

The Best Way to Stand Out Over the Competition

Which physician makes more money, the general practitioner or the heart specialist?

It's the heart specialist, of course.

There is a similar perception of greater value that operates in business. People trust and pay more for an expert in a field who has a well-defined, singular focus. A business that does not have this single-focus expertise won't attract customers as well as one that does.

What kind of focus am I talking about? You need to be an expert in one thing and be known for just that one thing.

Nike did so well with this approach that they are still known primarily for their athletic shoes. Even though the Nike brand now produces a variety of other athletic clothing, their diverse products are still grouped around their single core focus—shoes.

You can sell other services and products as long as they support your single focus of expertise.

When I started my business years ago, I enjoyed doing both business coaching and skills training for companies and conferences, so I billed myself as an "executive coach and trainer." Try as I might, my business sputtered until I followed the advice of a wise friend and chose just one thing as the focus of my expertise—executive coaching.

Business picked up steadily, and instead of falling off because of my focus on just that one area, the training side increased dramatically, too!

I found out that if you are known and trusted as an expert in your specialty, customers will also engage you to do the other things you do because they come to trust you, and they become willing to try your other offerings, too.

Lawyers are good at a single focus.

If you go to a law firm's website, you'll find all the lawyers listed there, each with a specialty beside his or her name. Notice that there is usually only one specialty per person. People have more confidence in someone who is an expert at one thing because they presume that the person knows just about everything there is to know about that thing.

So, if you are going to open a computer services store, what specific part of computer services will be your specialty? If you are going to be a marketing consultant, what specific kind of marketing will be your specialty? If you're going to sell clothing, what specific type of clothing will you sell—clothing about which you are an expert?

One of my very favorite breakfast restaurants sells just about every type of breakfast food you can imagine. What they are famous for, though, is their huge Dutch apple pancakes. They are experts at Dutch apple pancakes, AND they do a booming business in all those other breakfast dishes, too.

You want to become known as an expert in something and make that something the focus of your brand, the centerpiece of all your marketing.

Be aware that anytime you use the word "and" when you describe what you do, you have wandered away from your specialty focus.

I remember seeing a cartoon once with an image of a tired old guy leaning on the sill of a service window, waiting for a customer, all by himself in a hut beside the road.

The sign over his head read:

Fred's Fill Dirt & Croissants

You really don't want to be that guy.

Take action for traction: *How can you put the topic you just read about into action?*

Think about your expertise as it relates to your business idea as you work with these action items:

- What would be the specialty of the business you are considering launching? What one thing above all others would it deliver to customers and be known for?

- Some business owners are best at managing employees, and some are great at sales, while others are experts about the product or service that is sold. What would be your greatest personal expertise and specialty *within* your company?

- What else will you sell that supports your specialty? If your specialty is Apple computers, you would probably sell classes, accessories, and add-on software. Make a list of all the things you would sell in your business that would support your core product or service.

What Is Your Market?

Next, you need to figure out who your customers are—what your market is.

If you ask someone who has not given this enough thought, you will likely get an answer such as, "My market is anyone who would buy my product or service."

That is not really the best answer because it is way too broad and undefined, and you would have a hard time deciding where to focus your time, energy, and dollars to attract actual customers.

When your business specializes in something—as it should—you also want to specialize in who your customers are. In other words, you want to find out who your best customers are and mainly focus on them in your marketing efforts and service. They are most likely to buy from you and become repeat customers.

More about that in a minute, but first, your market must meet these three basic criteria, or it is not really a market at all.

1. *Your customers must want and need what you sell.*

    Before the iPod there was the music CD, and before the music CD there was the audiocassette, and before the cassette was the phonograph record, and before the phonograph record there were live musical performances.

Each of these venues gave people a way to hear their music in the best way for the times, and each of them dominated the marketplace and killed the competition for a while.

Customers will always put their money where their needs and emotional desires are, and whoever sells something that fulfills those needs and desires better than anyone else will reap the benefits.

What this also means is that even when you have a long-term, sustainable business, you will still have to innovate[38] and change over time to avoid becoming yesterday's top dog. You will have to keep refreshing your offering to keep customers' need and desire for it high.

Coffee[39] is a good example of something that has attracted sustained popularity over the long haul, but with a lot of innovation along the way.

Even though coffee is a deep, core piece of American culture, coffee marketers still have to innovate heavily, both about the evolving definition of coffee and about how to create the best and most interesting coffee experience for customers. Consider the amount of innovation that has occurred as we have gone from Maxwell House coffee in a can to the present-day Starbucks store offerings.

---

[38] http://www.forbes.com/sites/innovatorsdna/2012/06/04/are-you-an-innovative-entrepreneur/
[39] http://theoatmeal.com/comics/coffee

A simple cup of coffee was innovated into a double-double Caramel Macchiato.

When it comes to connecting with buyers, you have probably heard this saying: "He is such a good salesman, he could sell refrigerators to Eskimos."

The implication here is that the salesman is so good that he could sell people something they don't really need or want. Although we can wander from our actual need with a momentary impulse buy, people who don't have an emotional desire or need for what you are selling are not likely to buy it.

You won't do well with a tanning booth in the tropics, you won't have much luck selling raincoats in the desert, and it will be very hard to sell a swimming pool in New York in January or a Christmas tree in Dubai in July.

People must feel an emotional desire and a need for what you sell, or they aren't in your market.

2. *Your potential customers need to make up a big enough group to constitute a market.*

You probably won't find a flower store that just sells petunias. Many people like and buy petunias, but there aren't enough of those people to make up a big enough market to support your business with that flower alone.

Roses, on the other hand, are widely loved, and there are so many passionate rose lovers[40] that there are rose specialty catalogues, stores that sell nothing but roses, and rose sections within other stores. In this case, there are plenty of customers for roses—enough to constitute a market and to support a variety of businesses.

The Internet has also made it easier to invent and define new markets for many things because you can find your customers all over the world instead of being limited to your community or region. If you have something to sell, plus a laptop and Internet service, you're in business if you can reach enough people, no matter where you or they live, and your customers need only have access to delivery options.

---

[40] https://www.facebook.com/pages/Rose-Lovers/146634225374584

3. *Your customers must be able to pay your bill.*

I had a coaching client once who happened to be another business coach, and she first came to my door very disappointed. She had put a lot of time into developing a very creative and comprehensive six-month coaching program for start-up businesses that completely flopped when she went out and tried to sell it.

Feedback from her prospective customers was nearly unanimous—they all felt it would help them get off the ground, but it cost too much, and they couldn't afford it at this stage of their business development. They couldn't pay the bill.

So it was back to the drawing board, and my client realized that whatever services she offered to owners of start-ups would have to be priced very inexpensively. How to do that so she could still make a living was the question.

She ultimately decided to start a weekly business development coaching call for start-up owners for the tiny price of $40 a month. This was such a bargain, and it fit the budgets of start-ups so well, that she soon had a successful coaching call that drew more than 20 weekly callers. At that point she was making $200 an hour for her time, and her profit just got larger as more start-up owners came to the call.

She found a way for people to afford her services, and once she did that, enough people bought them to become a market for her.

Once you have determined that there is potentially a market for what you are proposing to sell, it is time to look more closely at that market to see where your business fits.

Market Research—
Not As Boring As It Sounds

You need to figure out if there is room to sell your particular product or service in what may be a very crowded marketplace, and you need to know how you can make a decent living doing that. To determine this, here are some free in-depth market research[41] tools you can use to find out where your business can fit and prosper.

Also, here is how to really use Google[42], your best friend every morning, noon, and night, to do more of that research.

Anything you want to know—nearly anything in the world—can be found through Google. You just need to ask the right questions in the search field. Asking the right questions means asking multiple questions about anything you need to know using every combination of words and phrases related to that basic core question that you can think of.

Google everything you can about your actual or potential competition. Who is selling this already? Where are they? Exactly what do they offer, and how do they sell it? Who is really good at it, and who is not? Who is the leader in this field, and why? What are they doing right, and what are the others doing wrong? Is the industry trending up or down? Is it growing or shrinking, hot or cold?

---

[41] http://www.entrepreneur.com/article/222489
[42] http://searchengineland.com/guide/how-to-use-google-to-search

One of the most important things you must research[43] relates to the business trends[44] in your industry. Does it have a lot of potential for growth and longevity? Is there a lot of innovation going on to keep it fresh and strong?

And, is the timing right?

You don't want to buy franchise number 40,000 from Starbucks or McDonald's—you want to buy one of the first hundred.

Ideally, you buy into your industry when it's taking off, not when it's leveling off or coming down. Or you could bring something disruptively new to a developed industry that will redefine it and send it back up on a new cycle of growth.

Think iPod.

You need to do additional market research, too. Google is a great place to start, but there are resources out there that allow you to really dig down and get a lot of good in-depth market information.

A good place to begin is by checking out government market and industry data. There is a lot of information to be had about businesses, industries, economic conditions, your potential customers, and your competition.

---

[43] http://www.entrepreneur.com/article/70518-1
[44] http://cocsbdc.org/2011/10-tips-for-staying-on-top-of-trends/

Some places to look include these websites:

> For economic indicators:
> http://www.census.gov/economic-indicators/
>
> For employment statistics:
> http://www.bls.gov/ces/
>
> For income and earnings:
> http://www.bls.gov/bls/wages.htm

You can also look into trade groups and publications for the industry you are considering, plus business magazines, books, and academic institutions.

Again, Google is your best friend. Type in a search question about anything you are looking for, and you are likely to find what you need to know.

Don't make a rookie mistake and stop on the surface, either, or just focus on the things that confirm what you want to hear. Don't stop digging and compiling until you get everything that is relevant.

Do your market research until you're sick of it, and then go do some more. The information you gather now will help you make an awesome business plan, and your business decisions along the way will only be as good as the foundation of knowledge and choices you put together at this point in your process, so take your time, get it all, and get it right.

As your search progresses, you're going to find out whether there's a place for your business as you imagine it now. If there is, all the information you have soaked up will coalesce, and the knowledge that you are really onto something will become clear at some point.

Or you may find that you have to tweak your original idea, play with it, and reshape it to make it just right to fill a need and fit the niche. I have to tell you that, most of the time, original business ideas benefit from being molded and reshaped somewhat so they are ready for prime time. The original idea is a great starting point from which a good business model can emerge.

Let's say your goal is to open a shoe store, and you find out that there's an empty storefront right next to a popular clothing store that doesn't sell shoes!

This would seem to be an ideal situation, but before you jump on the opportunity, you need to dig deeper and do some more research.

Is that open space there because nobody has seen the promise of it yet? Or is it there because others have tried what you're thinking about and have failed, and you haven't found out about that part yet?

Keep looking and keep digging until you know everything you can know about potential opportunities, including all pertinent history and potential pitfalls.

Don't let your emotions make decisions, and don't act until you're ready.

Now, let's say all your research proves out finally, and it turns out that you have really found your niche, the piece of the market where you can settle down and sell shoes all day long. That would be a fortunate and clear outcome for all your work.

That straightforward outcome sometimes happens, but oftentimes things aren't that immediately clear.

What Is Your Compelling Value Proposition?

Before you can start selling your product or service, you must define your value proposition[45]. Just because you have something to sell doesn't mean people will buy it. They must first perceive that it has compelling value for them.

It is not enough that your product or service has some general value to potential customers. To get them to actually buy from you means that the value must be compelling—it must be very strong—strong enough to trigger a sale and to make them choose you over your competition.

Let's say, for example, that you're thinking of opening a super-competitive business like a pizza delivery restaurant, and there are five other pizza joints in town. At that point, you know you have a complicated challenge. You'd better be able to find a way of doing pizza delivery that is more compelling to your potential customers than what the other guys offer, or your place will just be one in a crowd.

You must define your *compelling value proposition*, which is the answer to this question: what will make your product or service so compelling that customers will choose to buy it from you instead of from your competition? What will make you stand out as THE first choice?

---

[45] http://conversionxl.com/value-proposition-examples-how-to-create/

You need to define your value proposition clearly and specifically, and write it down so you can build your business around it, because your success will depend upon getting this right.

Is your pizza actually the best in the area? Do you have toppings or features that others don't offer? Do you differentiate yourself by your service instead of your product—"hot, delicious pizza to you in 10 minutes or you don't pay," for example?

What is going to make customers scroll or stroll right by those other pizza purveyors[46] and choose you?

Your need for a compelling value proposition holds true no matter what you are selling or where you are located.

At this stage of your exploration you must come up with a strong value proposition for what you are considering in order to know whether your business idea has any kind of chance of making it as a real business.

Once you have that, you are ready to explore further what you would need for this business—you're off to the races. Defining your value proposition will tell you a tremendous amount about whether your current thinking has real potential, so spend as much time and energy on it as you need to in order to nail this down and get it right.

---

[46] http://www.pizzatoday.com/departments/features/2013-top-100-pizza-companies-list/

Here is a good example of what a great value proposition can do for a business.

Some accountants[47] are employed by large firms, and other entrepreneur accountants work by themselves or in small practices.

The entrepreneur accountants usually set themselves up to do the same stuff as the corporate accountants, only on a smaller scale. Their value proposition is usually something around giving more personal and customized service to customers.

It sounds good on the surface, doesn't it? Who wouldn't rather have personal and customized service from an accountant, or from any other professional, for that matter?

But personal and customized service does not add up to a compelling value proposition when all the other thousands of entrepreneur accountants out there are saying the very same thing and promoting themselves in the very same way! That particular value is just skin in the game at that point—a starting point in the field, something everyone needs, and nothing that stands out.

Remember, a compelling value proposition is what makes you STAND OUT from your competition[48] in a way that pulls spending customers in your door. If it doesn't make you stand out and compel sales, you've missed the mark.

---

[47] http://www.forbes.com/sites/calebmelby/2011/06/17/brutally-honest-accountants-confess-to-being-boring/
[48] http://businesscasestudies.co.uk/business-theory/marketing/business-competitors.html#axzz2ybZmQqcU

I did some coaching work with a very sharp accountant who realized all this. She came up with a unique value proposition that created a breakthrough for her company.

In addition to doing the standard accounting work that so many other firms do at their offices, she has built a specialty by sending her accountants and bookkeepers to client companies at their locations at a moment's notice to do whatever work is needed. She helps them meet tight deadlines, plugs the gaps when employees leave or get sick, handles urgent surprises and problems, and relieves overwhelmed accounting staff. She is those clients' fire truck, their rescuer, and she will put whatever kind of accounting help they need in their offices within 24 hours of their call, for as long as it takes to get them back to happy.

That is what I mean by "compelling." Nothing is more compelling than seeing a fire truck pull up to your door when your house is on fire.

Putting together a powerful value proposition is not easy. If you try as hard as you can on your own and you cannot come up with a unique and compelling value proposition for your business idea, you might want to seek some professional help, someone like a business development coach or marketing expert. They can show you how to tweak your business idea so its value proposition springs into view, and then they will help you whittle it down to a sharp point.

Who Is Going to Sell What Needs to Be Sold?

Once you have your compelling value proposition, you are all set to use it to sell the socks off of whatever you are selling[49], but a crucial question remains to be answered: who is going to do that selling?

There are a lot of entrepreneurs with great talents, skills, and ideas whose efforts to build their businesses hit the wall when it comes to sales. Yet selling must happen, or you won't have a business at all. It is good to know right now how—and by whom—the selling will be done before you invest any more time or resources in your business idea.

This is a huge, big, honking deal because so few potential business owners know how to sell or have any interest in selling, and they so often sail off into their new businesses unequipped to bring in the revenues they will need to survive. They hire amateur salespeople, they invest in ineffective promotions, and they think people will come just because their door is open and the sign is up.

Until you figure out the selling part, your business dream needs to percolate some more.

I hear this all the time from entrepreneurs: "I hate to sell— I just hate to push people into anything. I have to sell, of course, but I hate it."

---

[49] http://theoatmeal.com/comics/sell_generation

This mindset will not produce abundant sales, and if that is the way you really feel about selling, it might stop you from starting your business at all. If you are smart, you are not going to sign up to do something you hate.

The best salespeople love to sell, and potential customers know when they meet you whether or not you are comfortable in the salesperson role.

Ah, I used the "salesperson" word. Made you flinch, didn't I?

The truth is, everybody is selling something all the time. Whenever you want something and ask for it, there is usually some selling involved. I need to borrow your tools because… I want to marry you because… Dad, can I use your car because…?

When you think about it, you really are a natural salesperson because you negotiate for things you want all the time.

Most people would say they hate to sell because their definition of a salesperson is the picture they have in their minds of a high-pressure used car guy pushing people around with slick sales tactics. Many people think "selling" means you have to manipulate people to get them to buy things, and since nobody wants to do that, they think they hate selling.

Fortunately, manipulating people out of their money is not what selling is about when you're doing it right.

I have a different perspective on selling: *a sale will happen when someone has enough information to know that he or she really wants what I have to sell.*

My job is not to persuade them to buy it but rather to find out through a conversation with them whether my product or service is right for them and whether they really want what I have to offer.

The true essence of sales, when it is done right, involves having a relaxed conversation with a potential customer that helps that person figure out whether he or she really needs or wants what you have. It is about testing for fit like trying on a suit; it is not about trying to push the person into something he or she doesn't want that isn't right.

If what you have is truly a fit, your discussion about it will stoke enthusiasm, and your prospective customer will buy right into it.

That conversation also gives you the opportunity to see if this prospect is really somebody you want to work with if what you offer is an ongoing service—someone who is a fit for you personally. Customers must be a fit for you, just as your product or service needs to be a fit for them, or you won't enjoy your work and will end up resenting them.

If you get what I'm talking about and learn to sell this way, many disasters will be avoided. The testing-for-fit approach takes all the pressure out of the interaction for both the seller and the potential buyer.

If you, the seller, are perfectly willing for people to walk away if they really don't need or want what you have, you are doing the right thing for them, and you will probably enjoy your interaction with them much more because there is no pressure. You will stay relaxed because you know that even though this person may say no, sooner or later people will come along who *do* want what you have to sell, who will buy, and who are great to work with. And because you know those future prospects will want what you have to offer, your conversations with people today will not carry a feeling of pushiness. A sale, when it happens, will occur much more naturally and easily.

Are there ways of presenting what you have to sell that are better than other ways? Yes indeed, and they are worth learning, but at the end of the day, selling is really about giving people the information they need about the benefits of what you have so they can decide whether or not they want to buy it.

Your job as a salesperson for your company—and all business owners are salespeople for their companies—is to stay in that relaxed mode all the time. This sounds easy, but most people find it extremely difficult in practice. If you can actually do it and stay out of your own agenda about your need for money or how you hate selling, sales will happen, and the money will roll in easily and abundantly.

It may be that you personally won't end up taking on a big sales role in your company. It may be that the right thing to do will be to hire others to sell for you. If, knowing what I just told you, you still don't want to sell every day—if it isn't a strength of yours—by all means find others who can and will do it for you in a thoroughly professional, effective way. If that is the way you want to go, you will still need to know enough about sales to adopt a sales approach that fits for you, and you will need to know how to hire and watch over the people who sell for you so they do it right.

There is a great book about this, and it will take you through everything you need to know about how to be an excellent, relaxed, and happy seller of your products or services, without pushing people around at all.

Go to Amazon.com and buy this book: *Six Secrets of Sales Magnets*, by Laura Posey and Will Turner.
                         http://amzn.com/1598012290.

Read it all the way through. This is a whole new way of thinking about sales and a whole new way of interacting with potential customers that will be much more profitable and enjoyable for you and your salespeople. It will also give you details about how to set up and run your sales operation.

Can You Make a Living That Meets Your Income and Lifestyle Needs?

This question about making a good living and having the life you want must have a satisfactory answer before you begin, or your business could turn out to be unsatisfactory in meeting your needs while you throw a lot of time and money into it.

Reading and acting upon the guidance in this book may have already given you a good feel for the answer to this question. There is one more thing you need to do, however, that will really paint a picture for you of what your business will likely look like and what its potential is to fund you and your lifestyle of choice.

You need to come up with a big, steaming pot of goals.[50]

You've set goals already, you say. But wait—not like this you haven't, and you probably don't have goals that are very specific for this particular decision.

The goals you need are definitions of destinations that you want to reach in your business, and in your life. They will also act as measuring points to let you know how you are doing along the way.

Sometimes it is fine in your personal life to just wander, to let the destination take care of itself while you enjoy the journey. Vacations can be great fun that way. Answering big existential questions like "Who am I?" or "What is my

---

[50] http://www.entrepreneur.com/article/225655

purpose in life?" absolutely requires lots of wandering around in an unplanned kind of way.

In business, though, we call a lot of wandering around past a certain point "winging it," and good things don't happen as often when you wing it as they do when you know where you're going. Every zig and zag you take while you figure things out on the fly costs time, money, and progress. It also makes the people who have to deal with you nuts.

Sitting there all by itself in your head at this point, your business idea looks so pretty and seems kind of simple, but how will this idea look when it connects up to the real world, and exactly how will you make that happen?

Some people jump right into a business without ever considering where they are going with it, but if you want a life that is more than the unstable result of random choices, you need some purpose[51] and design behind your business that will aim that business toward supporting you in the life you want.

The best way to find out about how to do this is to begin by getting some strong, specific goals in place, both for what you want your business to look like and for yourself personally. That way, you will have a really clear picture of what you want in your work as well as in your life.

---

[51] http://www.wikihow.com/Find-Your-Life's-Purpose

You must have both types of goals because your business and your life need to mesh well together for either one of them to work well individually.

If you don't have those two sets of well-defined goals working together, you will have competing priorities—being successful OR having a life, working all the time OR having the personal time you need. Harmonious business and personal goals take "either/or" decisions and turn them into "and/and" decisions. Being successful AND having a life. Putting in as many work hours as are necessary AND having the time off you need.

This place right here, where you are now, in this time of excited exploration about your business, is where you need to start making a habit of always thinking on two tracks—about your business and what it needs, and about you and what *you* need.

It is the only way both areas of your life will support each other.

Dual goals like that will allow you to measure opportunities and events that come your way in both areas. Does it fit with your business goals to do something personally *this* way or not? Does your business decision fit with your personal goals if you do *that* or not? Is the business or personal decision you're about to make good for both your work *and* your life?

Goals also keep you from getting sidetracked into time and money-wasting dead ends that could pull you off course.

When you don't really know where you are going, you are winging it, and you are very susceptible to hitting a lot of dead ends and U-turns because you are experimenting with everything in your business all the time.

Your head hums with possibilities, and all those options demand your attention and hide your direct road to success.

If you don't have a set of clear business and life goals, you're going to end up with an unfocused, experimental business and a patchwork quilt of a life.

Once you have compiled a list of your work and personal goals, you will see much more clearly how your proposed business would need to perform so you can reach all of them. You can do some research into the pay and lifestyles in the industry you are considering joining, too, and measure what you find out against your goals.

Each type of business has its own income and lifestyle features.

Lawyers can make a lot of money, but the climb to the top is very competitive and hard, often requiring that they give up large chunks of their personal lives for the work.

Owning a retail store is a dream for many, but you need money to buy in, and you are ultimately responsible for all the hours it is open and for everything about how it runs, from buying and stocking to managing the help to dealing with taxes and regulations.

Fishing charter captains might seem to have an ideal job to anyone who loves to fish, but their days are dictated by wind and weather, and by the recreational whims of tourists and impulse buyers. There is a lot of uncertainty, and the revenues are unpredictable.

When you have a set of very clear work and personal goals, you can look at them and compare them to the lives and incomes of people in your possible business. Then you will begin to know what you are signing up for and whether it will meet your needs.

If you discover through your research that others are prospering at some version of what you want to do to the level you desire, and that the trade-offs of that life are acceptable to you, you can proceed with more confidence into the business you are considering.

What Do You Bring to the Table?

A carpenter brings his toolbox to build you a house. What do you bring that would help you build your business?

This would be a good time to make some lists (hint, hint).

What personality traits[52] and skills do you have that would be helpful in business? What are your strengths? Are you good under pressure, good with people, good with money? Are you a good communicator, planner, or manager? Can you put together projects, take the long view, even inspire people? Are you enthusiastic, driven, or tenacious? Are you open, teachable, willing to learn? What previous useful experience do you have? Who do you know who might be a valuable contributor in any way to your business?

What are the things about who you are and what you can do that will help carry you where you want to go, and whom do you know who would be helpful to you?

Make a list of everything you can think of. These things are like money in the bank—they will lead you to actual money in the bank. Your skills, experience, contacts, and good communication abilities are working capital as surely as any coin or paper, and you need to know all about your strengths and advantages before you begin.

What have you got going for you that would be good for your business? Write it all down.

---

[52] http://www.livescience.com/41313-personality-traits.html

Following are some examples; be sure and add your own.

Can you:

- Communicate well
- Negotiate
- Get along well with others
- Inspire
- Lead
- Work hard
- Ask good questions
- Create and stay within budgets
- Keep your temper when provoked
- Guide and develop people
- Let go of relationships when you need to
- Clearly express what you want and expect
- Be consistent
- Lead a team
- Admit when you are wrong
- Persuade others, appropriately
- Make good policies

- Take charge
- Allow others to contribute to solutions
- Be on time
- Take responsibility
- Delegate effectively
- Take time off for non-work activities

Have you had experience (business or personal) with:

- Project management
- Organizational development
- Planning and scheduling
- Marketing
- Sales
- Technology
- Personnel management
- Money management
- Record-keeping
- Inventory control
- Training delivery
- Consulting or coaching

- Writing
- Publicity
- Research
- Computers and software
- Customer service
- Billing or accounts receivable
- Financial services
- Any other helping profession or service

Are you:

- Good with money
- Financially stable
- Emotionally steady
- Patient
- Willing to learn
- Good with time management
- Comfortable in social situations
- An effective networker
- A good listener
- Honest with yourself and others

- Able to praise people when they do good things
- Focused
- Persistent
- Kind
- Reasonable
- Direct
- Tactful
- Organized

Do you:

- Get the big picture; think forward
- Make good decisions
- Set goals (business and personal)
- Take care of your health and fitness
- Save money or invest
- Drive carefully
- Keep your promises
- Know lots of people
- Have high self-esteem
- Put effort into your relationships

- Collaborate well with others
- Know how to deal with difficult people
- Have good credit
- Have good ideas
- Respect different ways of thinking and being
- Think strategically
- Enjoy time off
- Give back to your community or profession
- Have a social life
- Have a hobby or special interest
- Have a BHAG—a Big Hairy Audacious Goal

Any and all of these things are helpful and transferrable to working a business, so I encourage you to add the ones that apply to your list, plus anything else about you and your experience that is a strength or accomplishment.

Keep this list.

Later, if you decide to set up a business, you can see from the list where you are strong, and you can also see as you go along where the gaps are that will need filling by others you can bring on who will be strong in those areas.

Take action for traction: *How can you put the topic you just read about into action?*

- The best next step to find out how your strengths play out in your life is to take the same strengths assessment used by employers to get to know candidates when they are hiring for positions. Go to *http://www.gallupstrengthscenter.com*, where you can take the free Gallup StrengthsFinder online assessment. The results will tell you about your top five strengths.

    Better yet, you can pay a reasonable fee and take the expanded assessment on that page that will give you in-depth reports about 34 of your measured strengths.

    This strengths assessment is an excellent guide for you when it comes to knowing what you do best and where you fit in the work world.

Don't Get Killed by the Internet

Another thing to think about while doing your research is that your competition might be anywhere in the world. People don't hesitate to shop on the Internet[53] to find more choices and save money, and overall they have less loyalty to their hometown businesses than in the past.

The Internet multiplies competition faster than rabbits breed.

Back in the day, before the World Wide Web changed everything, you could do very well with a local office supply store. Then the large office supply chains like Staples and Office Depot came along, and small local stores could not compete with big box prices and variety.

Soon enough, though, the big chains started into their own decline because consumers discovered the Internet marketplace, where they could price-compare and shop with any office supply provider anywhere in the world 24 hours a day.

Local markets have now become global markets.

So, one of the first things you had better figure out about any business idea you have is whether the infinite variety and competition of the Internet will stomp it flat when you try to do it.

---

[53] http://www.internetsociety.org/internet/what-internet

Do you know how your competition is using the Internet to compete with what you want to do? Do you fully know who your competition is in this bigger marketplace?

You'd better find out.

This means that you must expand your pre-business research regionally, nationally, and globally so you can be certain that you are getting into a business that isn't going to be killed by the Internet.

There are basically two ways to deal with Internet competition:

1. Sell a product or service online that can compete and win against many, many competitors.

2. Offer a product or service that all those potential competitors cannot provide online—something that still must be transacted locally.

Getting a haircut, a sit-down restaurant meal, or a physical therapy session are still local experiences, but customers use Internet search tools to find and compare those offerings, to make their purchasing decisions about them, and rate them.

Whatever business you are in, you will have to make it Internet-friendly in various ways.

You will also want to be careful about one of the biggest black holes of the Internet—getting into a product or service that is commoditized at prices you can't match.

Commoditized goods and services are those for which price is the biggest factor to the customer. The difference in price drives the sale, with the products themselves being viewed as mostly equal in value.

Three pens for a dollar beats two pens for a dollar.

From electronics to clothing, from medical testing to legal services, anything that can be sold online is being sold online.

I know people who had their logos designed in South Africa, their medical surgery done in India, their copy paper shipped to them from out of state, and the steaks they eat flown in from a company in Omaha.

So ask yourself, what's to keep someone online from delivering the same product or service as you, priced lower than you can offer, in ways that will put you right out of business?

You must come up with a complete and workable answer to that critical question if you want to avoid being run over by the Internet.

Doug Hickok

How to Pass the Technology Test

When cars first appeared in the world of horses and carriages, many businesses were thriving as they sold products and services to the horse economy. Most business owners at the time thought cars were a noisy, dangerous fad, not yet knowing what Henry Ford was planning up in Michigan.

A wave of cars soon filled the country, and before long, horses—and businesses related to horse transport—were out to pasture.

We live in a world in which waves of digitally based technology[54] roll over us constantly, with new devices and connections that are faster and faster all the time. These new tools for doing business are constantly burying the older ways of doing business, so you've got to stay on your toes and keep up.

There are still people, though, who haven't fully made the transition.

If you have any resistance to using the latest technology—computers, tablets, smartphones, mobile payment apps, the cloud—you had better get past that in a hurry, or technology will put you out to pasture just like cars retired the horses.

---

[54] http://socialdriver.com/2013/07/24/5-inspiring-examples-of-digital-technology-for-business/

It's not good enough to be nonresistant to digital technology, you must be highly proficient with and *enthusiastic* about it, and stay up with it as it quickly and constantly evolves.

Yesterday's business owners had to connect through the telephone or mail, write letters on typewriters and wait for them to arrive at their destinations, do a manual inventory count, advertise in newspapers, and pay for everything with checks using offline banking.

Today's business owners routinely use digital technology that would look like something out of a science fiction movie to the business owner of just twenty years ago.

You must now master a range of digital devices and skills, connect through social media campaigns[55], and run the customer service side of the business using real-time customer feedback to constantly maintain very high satisfaction levels. Government taxing authorities expect you to file e-returns, you can digitally monitor exactly what your salespeople or maintenance crews are doing in real time, the desktop publishing tools on your computer can design and publish your message instantly in multiple channels, and inventory control is computerized in systems that give you up-to-the-minute data for ordering, manufacturing, and shipping.

I could go on, but you get my drift.

---

[55] http://www.socialmediaexaminer.com/social-media-campaign-elements/

This accelerating digitization of business is not optional; it is absolutely necessary in everything you will do at your workplace.

Are you ready for that?

You must fully embrace it, or your business will be an antique from the moment you open it.

Who Is Along for the Ride?

It's almost time to get started with your business, but there are still a few things left to check off your prep list that are really important.

To start with, you wouldn't believe how many people go through all the steps of researching and setting up a business, and they don't factor in all the people they know who will have a strong, long-term influence upon them, and upon that business, for better or for worse.

Nobody builds and runs a business alone.

You have family and friends, partners and collaborators, supporters and detractors, and you might want to float this business-idea balloon out there in front of some well-chosen, important people in your life and see who pops it and who grabs the string. It will be a very interesting thing to do, and you will get a lot of feedback, some of it useful.

You will find out which of your close people will line up behind you so you have all the support you need, want, and deserve.

No matter how skilled, smart, and lucky you are, you really need support when you take on something as new and big as starting and running a business. Whether your need will be for money, advice, or just an encouraging word and a sympathetic ear, your network of close people who are genuinely there for you will be sources of important support if you ask for and accept it.

You also need to figure out if anybody close to you might directly or indirectly hold you back.

I have a friend who had spent her adult life working for other people, and she was tired of it. She had a good idea for a business and was getting more and more excited about it because all her research pointed toward the possibility that what she had in mind might really work.

Then one night the telephone rang. It was her mother, who proceeded to lecture her for 15 minutes about how foolish she was to take this chance.

Mother concluded by telling her she ought to go to work for the post office, for the security and the regular paycheck!

When my friend got off the phone, her face was white. There were tears in her eyes, and she said she felt as if she'd been hit. It was an awful experience for her to find out so clearly that her mother did not support what she was about to do—that Mother was likely to be a weight around her ankles instead of wind beneath her wings.

My friend did go on to discover that her husband, her kids, and most of her friends supported her completely in her new venture.

She just had to be careful around her mother.

Despite that painful experience, it was a good thing that she found out before she started who was with her and who was not.

You need to do the same thing—mobilize your support and find out who's on your team so you won't feel alone. This is a really big deal to take on, and you deserve the celebration, the good wishes, and all the practical advice and support that will be there for you when you need it from people who were there for you before your business launched—people who really care about you and how your life turns out.

It's Time for Action

Is there anything about starting a business that I may have missed here? If so, please go look into it thoroughly. Don't make your decision until your due diligence is done. My version of "done" may not be yours.

There could be information you need that is industry-specific or there might be issues of timing.

You will know when you are ready, so whatever it is that still needs to be done, write it down and do it. Go learn everything you need to know until you are ready, until you know for sure that now is the time for you to start a business of your own.

There is no shame in deciding not to do it, by the way..

There is as much value in learning what it is that you're *not* cut out to do as there is in finding out what you are totally ready and suited for. If this exploration and preparation process has left you in any doubt about proceeding, then listen to that hesitation.

Do also be sure, whatever you choose, that there are not any "shoulds" operating in your decisions about this. You know, when someone says, you "should" be this or do that, or when you hear yourself saying to yourself, "I should be more realistic and just go for a job with a good paycheck."

I have a friend who has a small sign on the wall: "I will not 'should' on myself today." It is a wonderful reminder.

"Should" is a word we use to try to convince ourselves that we need to do something that our instincts or emotions are not so sure about. You can know, if you find yourself using the "should" word during any of this pre-business process, that there is some kind of split going on between what you think and what you feel.

You need to have both your thinking and your feeling onboard in order to successfully do most anything in life, and that certainly includes starting a business. So don't proceed with that business until both your brain and your heart are behind it.

Doug Hickok

A Word About Fear

Fear is a natural, positive emotion that is often not well understood by the person experiencing it.

That's right; it is a positive, useful emotion, just like every other emotion. Just because it is really uncomfortable when you feel fear does not make it bad or something to be gotten rid of.

When you consider taking on a new business, it wouldn't be surprising if you feel fear about doing that at some point. You may call what you feel by a different name—anxiety, worry, concern, or nervousness—but it is fear. We give it other names to try to describe it in detail, and also to reduce its impact on us.

Here is where the useful part of fear comes in.

Fear has two basic healthy functions. It tells us when we are in danger, and it tells us when we are in unknown territory and might want to slow down.

You can see that you would want to know about both of those things, right?

Back in the early days of the human race, fear was very straightforward—there was a tiger looking right at you on the trail with visions of dinner in its eyes, or there was person coming at you, ready to smack you with a rock.

Fear makes sense in those obvious situations.

But today, the things that rightfully evoke fear are not always that obvious. It is harder to attach the fear we are feeling to a thing or event that is amorphous or somewhat undefined, like "a business," and thus the feeling does not seem as useful.

Just know that it is natural to fear big new ventures, important things that will change our lives in meaningful ways. That is when the "unknown territory" fearful response comes to visit—to get you to slow down, take it easy, and get used to the idea.

When you are in the initial phase of being in love with your business idea, you will have lots of emotional ups and downs, and fear, if it joins the parade, is there for a good reason, with a helpful message.

Go for It—Yes or No?

So it's time for a gut check.

If you know for sure that you are ready to start your own business, then it's time to do that. Read on for a few more useful ideas on your way to startup.

If you think you are still in decision-making mode about it, then here are some things to consider.

The first and most important is, how will you make this decision?

I have written about many of the things that are important for you to think about and do as you consider becoming a business owner, and you have had your own process about it all along the way.

How will you decide? There are many ways.

Some people are fearless and clear during this stage—they just know deep down that they are going to start that business, and all the rest is details. It's done except for the doing.

Some explore the entrepreneurial business idea in great detail, gathering information, researching everything they can find, working the possible scenarios, and taking a long time to decide. For them, the decision is really an open question until they have asked all their own questions and studied every answer. They are careful and measured about their decision.

Others are impulsive; they may or may not inform themselves about all the things they need to know, and they may tend to jump right in. Falling in love with the idea is their style, and they are fine with finding out if there is just the right amount of water in the pool after they have jumped off the diving board. "Failure" isn't really failure after all—it's learning, so onward.

Consider your other biases, too. If you are a rational thinker, you need to be sure to bring your feelings along.

If you feel first and then think, you need to be sure your thinking mind is not sitting in the back seat behind your feeling heart.

Making sure all the parts of you have a seat at the decision table leads to better outcomes and more peace of mind.

Can you decide one way now and then change your mind? Of course you can.

If your initial decision is to go into business and you change your mind later, it will become more complicated to stop the further you are into it. The absolutely most important thing, though, is that you make the *right* decision for yourself, whatever that is and whenever you know it. Don't let anyone else talk you into or out of anything, drag you down, or push you ahead.

There can be great value in running your ideas past some trusted advisors, but be very clear about their agendas before you do. If your mother wants you to get a job at the post office instead of running your business, she will not give you clear, impartial advice. If your dad is pressing you to take over the family business, he probably won't support other options you consider viable.

It can be good to check out your ideas with professional advisors, but again, be very aware of their biases. A financial advisor will have a different take on things than a banker, and a person who has a successful business of his own will give you different feedback than one who struggles. Business coaches are great resources if they are good at what they do.

Always consider the source.

If you have partners or family members who will have skin in your business, you will make this decision with them to some degree, giving appropriate weight to their input according to each person's role and importance to your potential business.

And finally, from me, some questions, the answers to which are of utmost importance to many people.

If you take on this business, will you be creating a life for yourself that matters, a life that is fulfilling and fun?

How will your business make the world a better place? Do you have guiding principles and values for your life, and for your business? What matters most[56] to you? Is the business you are considering in alignment with that?

What is your philosophy of life, and of work? Your business will reflect those things, whether or not you are clear about them. It is good to know now what they are so you can spot them later in your business environment and be able to see how they are affecting your success.

So we arrive at a defining moment.

You have thought about this business, researched and considered everything—held this idea up to the light—and you know a lot more than when that idea popped into your head.

It is up to you to decide what to do about it now.

Go take a walk, soak in the tub, or jog around the neighborhood. Talk to your dog, pat your wife, or write some more in your journal. Distract yourself or focus some more—whatever works for you to get into a knowing place from which you can decide.

If not knowing goes on and on, then that is your answer. Anything but a yes is a no. "I think maybe I could do it" is not yes. Making endless pros and cons lists is not a yes. Putting off the decision is not a yes.

You will know when the answer is yes. You just know it, no matter what other feelings you might be having about

---

[56] http://www.psychologytoday.com/articles/201404/reinvent-yourself

it. You might be scared to death by this great leap you are taking, but you know what yes feels like even so. Think back to the other things you just knew about, and see what your knowing is now.

Anything but a yes is a no.

Go for it if the answer is yes—all your other concerns about it will have answers and the experience will be full of learning and growth.

Don't do it if the answer is no, or if the answer is anything but yes. Instead, go find out what would make you say yes and do that.

Congratulations! Now What?

You are joining the ranks of the many entrepreneurs doing good work in the world—some of the most talented, interesting, and successful people on the planet. They—and you—are willing to take bigger risks in exchange for bigger possible payoffs to have more control over their lives. This means you have courage, and if you dedicate yourself to learning whatever you need to know to do your business right, you and your business will both thrive.

Your process so far from initially having your business idea to being ready to move forward to build it has involved a lot of considering, thinking, mulling, and furrowing of your brow if you are like most people. You have done a lot of inner processing along with all the outer researching, exploring, and discussing that was so necessary to bring you to this point.

If you did it right, there was a lot of inner and outer work.

Your next step toward Opening Day for your business is step two—setup—where you plan your launch and put together all the parts of your business so it is ready to open.

This will be a time for more action, but the action still needs to include a fair share of inner with the outer, a good match of thinking, feeling, and sensing along with the doing.

This will be an intense and busy time.

Keeping your wits about you as you talk to your banker about the loan on the phone while the carpenter saws out a wall behind you and a job applicant fills out the form out on the stoop will be good training for the day when you open your very own complex, demanding, and wonderful business.

So right now, go ahead and be excited. Be very excited, because the paintbrush is in your hand, and the canvass of your life has never been so ready for bold strokes and bright colors as it is right now.

How to Succeed with Your Great Business Idea

About the Author

Doug Hickok is the President of Happy Workplace Consulting Group. He has more than twenty years of experience as an executive coach and communication expert specializing in leadership development.

Doug is a Certified Imago Educator (psychology and communication) and a nationally known author, trainer, and speaker. In addition to writing this book, he is also the author of the Amazon best-seller, *The Pursuit of Happiness at Work*.

Doug has taught in the Executive Education program at the Management Institute of the Robins School of Business, University of Richmond, in Richmond, Virginia. He is also an executive coach for The Honor Foundation, an organization that prepares Navy Seals for their transitions from the military into civilian business life.

Doug Hickok is a member of the International Association of Coaching, the Association for Talent Development, and the Academy of Management.

He lives with his wife Betsy in Annapolis, Maryland.

How to Succeed with Your Great Business Idea

Feel free to contact Doug for business assistance, or with questions and feedback about this book.

CONSULTING GROUP

Contact information:

Doug Hickok, President,
Happy Workplace Consulting Group

Email: doug@myhappyworkplace.com

Company website:
www.myhappyworkplace.com

> *A happy workplace inspires people to do their best work, which makes the companies that employ them exceptionally profitable and stable.*
>
> *At Happy Workplace Consulting Group we join with company leaders to build happiness-based success into their organizations at all levels, as a culture and a practice.*

Client Endorsement

Dear Doug,

I can't praise your book enough. I found it to be clear, well written, well organized and very instructive. It was challenging and thought provoking without being intimidating.

The timing of reading it was perfect for me.

The book helped me affirm my both my decision to create my business and the strengths I bring to the table. I also further clarified my niche, and I have a compelling value proposition for my service.

In addition, yesterday I was presented with the possibility of a partner or a loan from a friend, and your book helped me think more deeply about those options.

I would greatly value the opportunity to work with you further.

Yvonne C.
Richmond, Virginia

www.ingramcontent.com/pod-product-compliance
Lightning Source LLC
Chambersburg PA
CBHW061650040426
42446CB00010B/1674